ART AND HISTORY
SAINT PETERSBURG

BONECHI

Publication created and designed by: Casa Editrice Bonechi
Editorial management: Monica Bonechi
Graphic design: Manuela Ranfagni
Cover: Manuela Ranfagni
Image research: Monica Bonechi
Videopagemaking: Anna Baldini
Translation: Paula Boomsliter

Texts: Pavel Kann *and* Rita Bianucci
Text page 119: Giovanna Magi

Design for cover and pages 12-13: Sauro Giampaia
Map (inside cover): Stefano Benini

© Copyright by Casa Editrice Bonechi - Florence - Italy
E-mail: bonechi@bonechi.it - Internet: www.bonechi.com

Printed in Italy by Centro Stampa Editoriale Bonechi, Sesto Fiorentino (FI).

The *photographs that are property of the Casa Editrice Bonechi photographic archives were taken by* Marco Bonechi, Monica Bonechi, Yuriy Bykovskiy, Vladimir Denisov, Daniil German, Eugenij German, Aleksandr Kascnizkiy, *and* Vladimir Melnikov.
Other photographs are property of the Casa Editrice Aurora photographic archives, TASS, and APN.

Also collaborating were:
Courtesy of AVN: pages 16 bottom right, 77 top, 111 bottom, and 117 top and the three images at the bottom of the page.
Vladimir Melnikov: pages 13 top, 116 bottom, and 127 bottom.
Natalia Razina: page 109 (box), bottom and center.
© 2004 Russian State Museum of Saint Petersburg: *pages 5 second from the top, 6 center and bottom, 12 lower left, 31 center, 109 (box) left, and 117 the three center images.*

ISBN 88-476-1467-8

* * *

*I*n the beginning, the city on the Neva was called Saint Petersburg. After the outbreak of World War in August 1914, it was renamed Petrograd and, following the death of Lenin in 1924, Leningrad. Since 6 September 1991 it has been again called by its original name.

THE ORIGINS

At the start of the 2nd millennium AD the region of what is now Saint Petersburg belonged to the ancient Novgorod, whose warriors had repeatedly fought to repulse foreign raids on their territories: in 1240, led by Prince Alexander, they defeated the Swedes who had landed at the mouth of the Neva. In memory of the victory, Alexander Prince of Novgorod was attributed the appellative "Nevsky"—that is, "of the Neva"; he was later canonized and listed among the saints of the Russian Orthodox Church. In the early 17th century the region returned to the Swedes and Russia's development suffered for the lack of outlets to the sea: the shores of the Black Sea were held by Turkey; the Baltic Sea (including the Gulf of Finland) was the dominion of the king of Sweden. Communications routes and political relations with the seafaring traders and western European countries were interrupted. And while it is true that there was the port of Arkhangelsk on the Beloye More (White Sea), it is also true that it was closed many months of the year by ice and was difficult to reach.

PETER I AND "HIS" CITY

During the war against Sweden (1700-1721), the originally Russian lands on the shores of the Black Sea were again conquered under Peter's leadership. In 1703, Peter I brought in tens of thousands of serfs from all over Russia to build, at the mouth of the Neva river, the fortified city and port that was destined to become the country's capital. Peter wanted to call it Saint Petersburg; that is, "City of Saint Peter" after the apostle holding the keys to Paradise after whom the

founder was named. According to the czar, in fact, Saint Petersburg was the key for opening Russia to Paradise (that is, the Baltic), to prosperity, and to power.

At the time, Saint Petersburg was the only large city in the world in which construction was conducted in accordance with a pre-established urban plan. Differently from Moscow, with its traditional medieval development in concentric circles and narrow streets, the major arteries of Saint Petersburg were laid out in accordance with modern city planning criteria. Peter ordered study of housing projects for people of different social conditions: the needy, the well-to-do, the aristocrats. In 1714 the czar prohibited construction, in the city, of wooden buildings; he also decreed that throughout the country erection of stone buildings be stopped and that all the stonemasons, brick-makers, and masons—with their tools— be sent to Saint Petersburg. The city on the Neva was to have only buildings in masonry. In the meantime the cannons were thundering: the Battle of Poltava (1709) marked a turning point when the new Russian army won out over the troops of King Charles XII of Sweden. In 1710, following other victories, the front was finally distanced from Saint Petersburg and in 1712 the city was proclaimed capital of Russia.

STRUGGLES FOR POWER AND ARTISTIC FLOWERING

The death of Czar Peter I saw the beginning of a long series of palace intrigues plotted with ease by various groups of nobles. The throne was held, in succession, by Catherine I (1725-1727), Peter II (1727-1730), Anna Ivanovna (1730-1740), Ivan Antonovich (1740-1741) . . . During these backstairs struggles, in the years from 1728 to 1732, Moscow returned to being the temporary capital. Following the Muscovite parenthesis, Saint Petersburg saw erection of numerous palaces (including the Winter Palace) and churches (like Saint Nicholas' Cathedral); new industries were established (among which the imperial porcelain factory) and new educa-

Peter I

Catherine I

Elizabeth Petrovna

The Winter Palace

Drawings by Sauro Giampaia

tional institutions were founded (like the Academy of Arts).

In 1741, after another palace coup, Peter I's daughter Elizabeth ascended the throne and remained in power for twenty years. Years of unrestrained fetes, balls, and carnivals of a splendor without precedent in the history of the Russian court. Elizabeth was succeeded, for just six months, by Peter III, who was deposed by his wife Catherine and his allies of the Imperial Guard; when he was assassinated, only a few days later, his widow Catherine II, "the Great," ascended the throne. The empress, who corresponded with Voltaire, raised Russia to the world level in arts and literature, promoted the Neoclassical revival in the capital, and extended the empire with her victorious campaigns in Poland and Turkey. Although she had a name as an illuminated ruler, following the French Revolution she became more conservative and opposed any innovation inspired by that event.

In the late 18th century the exuberant Baroque style, which had as its maximum exponents Bartolomeo Francesco Rastrelli (the Catherine Palace at Tsarskoe Selo, the Winter Palace, and other buildings) and Savva Chevakinskiy (Saint Nicholas' Cathedral), thanks to Catherine II gave way to the reserved, rigorous Neoclassicism of Giacomo Quarenghi (Academy of Sciences), Ivan Starov (Tauride Palace), and later Carlo Rossi (General Staff Building), Andrei Voronikhin (Cathedral of Our Lady of Kazan), Andrei Zakharov (the Admiralty), and other masters.

The reign of Paul I, the unbalanced son of Catherine II, was brief (1796-1801). Years of paltry and militaristic ordering of the daily life of the city, which had become a huge military barracks, aroused public hostility: Paul I was killed in the Mikhailovskiy Castle by a group of conspirators. The throne was ascended by Alexander I, party to the planning of the regicide.

THE 19TH CENTURY

The salient moments of the first quarter of the 19th century were the patriotic war of 1812 and the Decembrist rebellion of 1825.

Napoleon's invasion of Russia roused public spirit: in the capital, volunteers signed up amidst the enthusiasm of the citizenry. The troops—serfs—fought valiantly in the hope that once the invading forces had been defeated they would have won their coveted freedom. Napoleon's army was almost completely destroyed and in 1814, to welcome the victorious troops, a wooden arch of triumph was built at the edge of the city: the Narva Gate. Later, the Alexander Column was raised as a monument to Russia's military glory.

The patriotic fervor aroused by the war against Napoleon was followed by significant acquisitions in national culture, the arts, and architecture, and by strong social ferment. The Decembrist rebels called themselves the "sons of 1812." The flags of victory inspired the genius of Russia's greatest poet,

Проспектъ въ верхъ по Невѣ рѣкѣ отъ Адмиралтейства
и Академіи Наукъ къ востоку.

Alexander Pushkin. The finest minds of the Russian aristocracy, the great majority of whom were former combatants, were not indifferent to the sufferings of the populace. They were planning a revolt when the sudden death of Alexander I and the following interregnum spurred them to act immediately. On 14 December 1825, the insurgent officials (later known as the "Decembrists" or "Dekabrists") set out to array their regiments in the square facing the Senate in the hope of convincing the organ to abolish serfdom and proclaim a republic. But by the time the rebel forces reached the square the Senate had already sworn loyalty to Nicholas I, Alexander I's brother; the Decembrists felt it would not be possible to force the Senate to an act of abjuration. As evening fell, Nicholas I ordered the government troops to open fire, and the cannons thundered again.

Russia's defeat in the Crimean War (1853-1856) highlighted the corruption and impotence of feudal Russian society. In this situation, pressed on also by the peasant uprisings, Czar Alexander II abolished serfdom. Capitalistic economics took off; in Saint Petersburg, new factories were built and the older ones enlarged.

THE OCTOBER REVOLUTION AND THE FALL OF THE ROMANOV DYNASTY

In Russian history, 9 December 1905 is known as "Bloody Sunday." On that day the czar's troops fired on a peaceful demonstration of workers heading toward the Winter Palace to implore the czar's protection against the intolerable acts of oppression perpetrated by their employers. About a thousand workers and their family members were killed and about two thousand were injured. The ingenuous faith of the workers of Saint Petersburg and indeed of all of Russia in the czar was transformed into implacable hate of all manifestations of czarism. The revolution of February 1917 drove out the autocracy.

Upon his return from exile, Vladimir Lenin exhorted the Bolshevik party to lead the populace in the next stage: the Socialist revolution. The insurrection of October 1917, with the battle-cruiser Aurora that on 25 October (7 November according to the new calendar) shot salvoes to give the signal for the assault on the Winter Palace, led to the victory of the Socialist revolutionaries.

Czar Nicholas II abdicated and retired with his family to Tsarskoe Selo, whence he was taken, with his wife and five children, first to the Siberian city of Tobolsk and then to Ekaterinburg, on the eastern slopes of the Urals. Here, in 1918, they were all assassinated, together with the family doctor and some of the servants, by the guards holding them prisoner. They were buried in a pauper's grave.

There followed the harsh, bloody years of the civil wars and World War I;

Catherine II "the Great"

The Great Poet Pushkin

Saint Isaac's Cathedral

Nicholas II

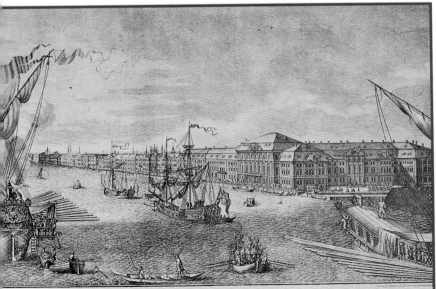

Vue des bords de la Neva en remontant la riviere entre l'Amiraute et les batimens de l'Academie des Sciences

Drawings by Sauro Giampaia

The Cruiser Aurora

The poet Anna Akhmatova

The composer Dmitri Shostakovich

Saint Petersburg, which in 1914, under pressure from the nationalists, had seen its name "Russified" into Petrograd, in 1918 was deprived of its status as capital in favor of Moscow.

In the years from 1921 to 1924, in order to revive the economy and cope with the discontent of workers and farmers, Lenin launched his New Economic Policy (NEP), which reinstated individual profit and freedom in economic dealings. The close focus demonstrated by Trotsky and the People's Commissar for Education Lunacarsky in regard of all the manifestations of the spirit favored the start and development of experimentation in all forms of art (this was the period of Mayakovsky, Kandinsky, Malevich, and the "street artists").

In 1924, at Lenin's death, Petrograd was renamed Leningrad. In 1927, power shifted into the hands of Stalin and the atmosphere changed radically. The city participated in achieving the objectives of the five-year plans, becoming one of the country's major industrial centers. Jealous of their heritage, the citizens did everything possible to preserve and develop the cultural traditions of the city, with its celebrated theaters, museums, and libraries, while construction went on under a new urban plan. Between 1934 and 1938, Stalin's "purges" eliminated—quite often physically—the dissidents and opponents of the regime, and many only suspected of such crimes.

THE SIEGE OF THE CITY (1941-1944)

The outbreak of war 22 June 1941 marked the beginning of a period of further suffering and anguish. The Nazi troops advanced rapidly and on 18 July the city was bombed for the first time.

By 8 September, the Nazi troops had surrounded the city; here began a

siege that lasted almost 900 days. During those interminable and terrible days every square kilometer was, on the average, hit by 324 incendiary bombs and 483 artillery shells.

Held under siege, tried by hunger and the cold, without water or electricity, harassed by artillery fire and aerial bombings, the citizenry resisted. Concerts and public poetry readings were held. And finally, on 18 January 1943, the siege was broken. A year later, in the battles of 14 and 27 January 1944, the troops at the front slowly drove back the German armies.

The heroism of the civilians and soldiers is remembered in the Moskovskiy Park and gardens along the sea embankment, built after the war, and in the monument in Victory Square with its 48-meter obelisk, taller even than the Alexander Column. In Insurrection Square soars the granite obelisk in honor of the "Hero City," while the Piskarevskoe Memorial Cemetery complex pays homage to the sacrifices sustained by the population. The victims, in those 900 days of siege, were practically innumerable: the most reliable estimate is one million dead.

FROM THE POSTWAR PERIOD TO OUR TIMES

Three years after the death of Stalin in 1953, Nikita Khrushchev denounced the dictator's crimes and paved the way to "the thaw." Following years in which hopes of freedom alternated with harsh repression under various Party secretaries, 1985 saw the election of Mikhail Gorbachov, who, with his policies of glasnost (transparency) and the famous perestroika (reconstruction), the launched that dissolution of the old Soviet Union that was concluded in 1991. In that same year, the ancient capital of the czars, the historical center of which UNESCO in 1990 included in UNESCO's list of World Heritage Sites, again took on its original name of Saint Petersburg.

The Piskariovskoe Memorial Cemetery

The dome of Saint Isaac's Cathedral seen from the Neva

Modern buildings along the Neva

The Neva near Decembrists' Square

The Movable Bridges on the Neva

A spectacle not to be missed, when the bridges open! Every night from May to September, when the bite of the ice relents and the waters of the Neva again run freely among the many islands at its mouth, Saint Petersburg regales tourists with a singular spectacle and the curtain rises on an extraordinary show: a sort of dance on the immense stage of the river, with the bridges as protagonists. Beginning at 1:55 AM, the enormous center sections begin to lift one by one: like luminous arms reaching up to the heavens, they seem to extend a welcome to the ships that, after a day's halt, again begin to move along the majestic currents of the Neva.

At 4:50 it's all over—but for anyone who has witnessed it, certainly an unforgettable memory.

THE PETER AND PAUL FORTRESS

*A*t the widest point of the mouth of the Neva, on Zayachy Island (Island of the Hares), there were built fortifications and decorative and other constructions that gave rise to the Peter and Paul Fortress, one of the most significative masterpieces of Saint Petersburg and the original nucleus of the city. The fortress in fact originated as a bastion for defense of the outlet to the Baltic Sea conquered by Russia.

The fortress played an important role in the victory of the October 1917 revolution. The same day as the October Revolution, the fortress passed into the hands of the insurgent populace. The weapons in the arsenal were distributed to the Red Guards, composed of workers; the fortress became the headquarters of the insurrection whence were directed the military actions.
In 1924, the Peter and Paul Fortress became a museum.

The Fortress with the Cathedral of Saints Peter and Paul, the Neva Gate, and the Commandant's Pier. In the box, a view of the city with the fortress in the background, in an etching by A. Zubov (1727).

On this page, the Fortress with the Cathedral of Saints Peter and Paul, seen from the northwest.

THE FORTRESS

The fortress was built very rapidly in 1703, spurred on by the fear that the Swedish navy and foot soldiers, the latter stationed at forward positions north of the city, might have attacked. The site of the fortification as chosen by Peter I and turned out to be felicitous: the cannons on the ramparts blocked access to the city not only from the Bolshaya (Great) Neva (as that part of the river that runs from the Liteynyy Bridge to the mouth of the river in the Gulf of Finland is often called), but also from its lesser arms: the Malaya (Small) Neva and the Bolshaya Nevka. But that original fortress in packed earth provided insufficient defense, and works for construction of a stone fortress began in 1706. Building went on for 35 years and only in 1740 were the new masonry walls raised 12 meters above the level of the Neva.
In 1780 the fortress, as was said at the time, "was clad in stone"; that is, it was faced on the side toward the Neva in the granite slabs we still see today.

The Mint

The Mint, moved from Moscow to Saint Petersburg by decree of Peter I in 1724, coined the currency of the Russian Empire. The Mint building (probably designed by A. Porto) was built inside the Fortress in about 1802. From 1876 onward, the Saint Petersburg Mint was the only place in the empire that produced metal coins. In 1921 it began coining Soviet coins and producing the official decorations and medals conferred by the Soviet Union and souvenir and commemorative coins and medals.

The dome of the Cathedral of Saints Peter and Paul.

Trubetskoy Bastion

In the 18th century the fortress was the place of detention for the sons of the Russian people who rose in revolt against autocracy and serfdom. It was here that the protagonists of the Decembrist revolt, Dostoevsky, Trotsky, Bakunin, Gorky, and many comrades of Vladimir Lenin were imprisoned. Most of these people were held in the prison built in the early 1870's in the Trubetskoy Bastion. Since 1924 the prison has been a **museum**.

Sand sculptures on the Fortress beach.

The writer Fyodor Dovstoevsky.

One of the turrets along the bastions.

Peter Gate

The most widely used entrance to the fortress is that to the east, on the Kamennoost-rovskiy (formerly Kirov) Prospekt side. Past the arch built in 1740, called Ivan's Arch, we find the Peter Gate: a single arch surmounted by a striking attic with a curved pediment decorated with volutes. It is the work of the architect Domenico Trezzini, dated 1717-1718. In practice, this is the only historical monument in the Fortress area that has come down to us in its original semblance. The parts of the old decoration that have been preserved are the **wooden bas-reliefs** by Pineau of ancient knights' armor and the god of Sabaoth in the clouds by Nicholas Pineau. Interesting the wooden bas-relief by K. Osner depicting the legend of the astrologer Simon Magus felled by the prayer of the Apostle Peter, an allegory of the defeat of the Swedish by Czar Peter I's troops. Above the arch is an imposing **two-headed eagle** in lead, dated 1720, the official emblem of the Russian Empire.

The niches shelter the **statues of Bellona**, goddess of war, on the right, and **Minerva**, on the left, allegories of Peter the Great's military and political genius.

The wall of the fortress in which the Peter Gate opens is 19.2 meters in thickness.

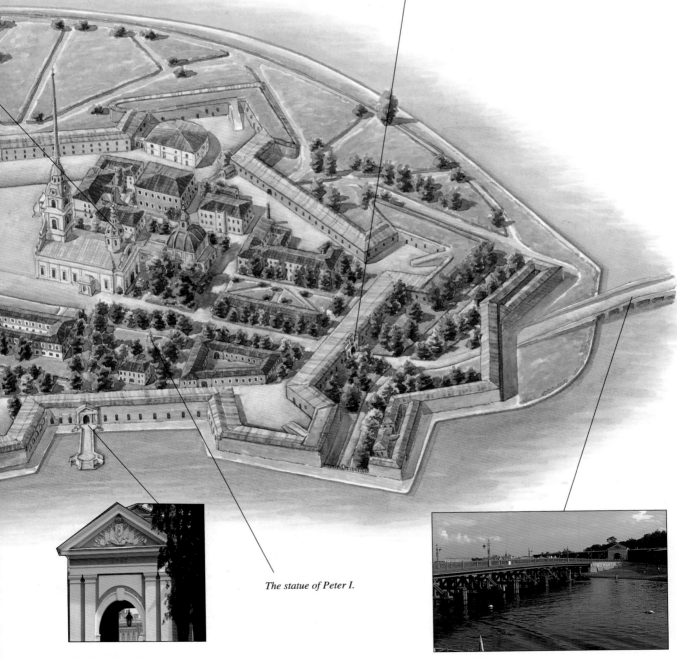

The statue of Peter I.

The Neva Gate (inner facade).

Ivanovskiy Bridge and the Ivanovskiy Gate.

THE CATHEDRAL OF SAINTS PETER AND PAUL

At the center of the fortress is its most important architectural monument: the Cathedral of Saints Peter and Paul: begun in 1712, it was built to plans by and under the direction of the architect Domenico Trezzini.

In elegant Baroque style, the facade of the building presents a bell tower, on several orders, culminating in a daring **spire**. Topped by an **angel holding a cross**, the gilded, needle-shaped spire lends a special feeling to the entire city skyline. With its 122.5 meters height, the cathedral was the tallest building in Saint Petersburg until the television tower (316 meters) was built.

On these pages, the Cathedral of Saints Peter and Paul and the building housing Peter I's boat.

The Czar's Boat

As we enter of the Fortress, near the west entrance to the Cathedral, we find a modest building (by the architect A. Wist, 1761), in which Peter I kept his boat, known to history as the "Grandfather of the Russian Fleet." Today, the boat is on display at the Naval Museum on Vasilevskiy Island.

The interior, divided into a nave and two aisles by pink and green pilasters ending in rich Corinthian capitals, is distant from the architectural canons of the traditional Russian Orthodox church: even the great wooden iconostasis gleaming with gold, a precious woodcutting work dating to about 1720, and the likewise gilded and elegant *pulpit*, are in the imaginative Baroque style. The cross-vaults are adorned with valuable frescoes and decorations, and above the presbytery there rises the dome, resting on a high tambour. The czar attended the religious rites on the platform surmounted by its baldachin. The cathedral hosts the **tombs of the czars of the Romanov dynasty**, from Peter I onward; the only exceptions are Peter II and Ivan VI. Interesting the sarcophagi of the tombs of Alexander II and his wife, made in the marble works of Peterhof from two monoliths, the first a block of jasper from Altai and the second a block of rhodonite from the Urals. Right of the iconostasis is the **sepulcher of Peter I**; the position was chosen by the czar in person. Since 17 July 1998 the ashes of the last czar, Nicholas II, his wife, children, doctor, and three servants, all of whom fell under the Bolshevik fire of 1918, have been conserved here. In the **grand-ducal mausoleum**, built in the early years of the 20th century east of the cathedral, are buried many princes of the Romanov family.

The interior of the cathedral and, below, the sepulcher of Peter I.

The End of the Romanov Dynasty

Nicholas II Romanov was born in 1868 at Tsarskoe Selo. He was the first son of Czar Alexander II and his Danish wife Maria Fyodorovna; he ascended the throne in 1894, the year of his father's death. This affectionate husband and father followed a policy as reactionary as that of his predecessors—but he was not at their equal. The first 10 years of his reign were calm, and everything considered Russia enjoyed considerable industrial development. In 1904-1905, defeats at the hand of Japan caused serious political and social unrest. The country saw peasant uprisings and strikes and mutinies by soldiers and sailors, all of which were harshly repressed; even the middle classes and a goodly number of the aristocracy supported Western-style laissez-faire policies. In 1906, Nicholas II created the State Duma (legislature) but then did everything in his power to make it ineffective. When the 1917 Revolution broke out, the czar abdicated in favor of his brother Mikhail, who renounced the throne and thus decreed the end of the Romanov dynasty and the Russian empire. Sentenced to house arrest at Tsarskoe Selo with his wife and five children, the czar was later taken with his family to Ekaterinburg, where they were all killed by the Bolsheviks on 16 July 1918 and buried in a common grave. The Russian Orthodox Church canonized Russia's last czar in 2000.

Czar Nicholas II and his wife Alexandra Fyodorovna, with their five children.

Drawings by Sauro Giampaia

THE CENTRAL BOULEVARD

The boulevard leading from the Saint Peter Gate to the cathedral is lined with squat buildings: on the right, the **artillery depot** dating to the early 19th century; on the left, the **Engineers' House**, built in 1740 for the team of engineers participating in construction of the fortress and today hosting an exhibit illustrating daily life in Saint Petersburg before the Revolution.

Further on, past the Engineer's House in an area landscaped as a garden, stands the modern **statue of Peter the Great**, a 1991 work by Mikhail Chemiakin.

After the garden, and by this point alongside the cathedral, we come to the **Commandant's House**. At one time, this beautiful Baroque building was the residence of the commander of the fortress although a part of it was utilized as a courthouse: many political prisoners were tried here, among whom the Decembrist rebels. Today, the building houses a **museum of local history**.

The statue of Peter the Great in a garden along the central boulevard and, right, the grand-ducal mausoleum.

17

THE NEVA GATE

Facing the south side of the cathedral, an arch in the walls opens out onto the banks of the Neva. And here we can admire one of the fortress' finest constructions, the grandiose Neva Gate built by the architect Lvov in 1787.

Faced in granite slabs, the gate was designed as an arcade on double columns united by heavy blocks of stone. The interior facade of the gate is less imposing but invested with severe elegance.

It was through this gate that the condemned prisoners passed at night from the **Commandant's Pier** to the Schlüsselburg or to the Lisiy Nos (Fox's Nose) Fortress overlooking the Gulf of Finland, where the death sentences of the Czarist court were carried out.

On the Commandant's Pier there rises the mass of the **Naryshkin Bastion**, from which, traditionally, a single cannon shot is fired every day exactly at noon.

THE FORTRESS BEACH

In summer as in winter, day and night, this is one of the most popular sites in the city; the "regulars" are mainly young citizens of Saint Petersburg, but they are not alone. The reasons are many and varied. First of all, the beach offers an incomparable panorama; the visitor's gaze ranges from the Field of Mars with the white profile of the Marble Palace to the Palace Embankment on which stand out, like the jewels in a necklace, the gleaming buildings of the Hermitage, while above the roofs the Alexander Column and the spire of the Admiralty seem to reach up to touch the sky. Further right, the tip of Vasilevskiy Island, unmistakable with its red Rostral Columns and a "flash," reminiscent of Magna Graecia, of the temple-like building of the former stock exchange, today the Naval Museum.

And what better standpoint, with three bridges in clear evidence, to watch their nightly opening? Then, of course, if it happens to be the period of the "white nights" (from mid-June to early August, when the sky is illuminated all night long), the spectacle is truly unique.

On this beach, which has become a favorite spot for relaxation and entertainment, people make music, dance, sing, and toast, often among artistic and truly incredible sand sculptures. Favorite pastimes here are sunbathing and swimming—and not just in the summer: many daredevils, in fact, break the ice for a "fortifying" dive into the freezing winter waters of the Neva. The beach is the starting point for romantic walks over the frozen river or expeditions to points in mid-river to fish through holes cut in the ice.

The inner facade of the Neva Gate and the beach, with its wonderful view of the Palace Embankment.

The fortress, with its beaches and parks, is crowded in summer and winter alike and offers a myriad of recreational facilities and opportunities for simple relaxation.

Artillery Museum

North of the island that hosts the Peter and Paul Fortress, in the immense Alexandrovsky Park, a great red-brick horseshoe building was once the city's arsenal and today is the home of the Artillery Museum.

From the weapons of the Middle Ages to those of World War II, from uniforms to flags, from cannons to armored tanks: a visit to this museum will certainly be rewarding, and the visitor will certainly come away with a souvenir photo of himself alongside a unique artillery piece . . .

The Cabin of Peter the Great

On the right bank of the Neva, across from the Summer Garden, at No. 6 of the Neva Embankment, there rises a humble building, the only one remaining from the city's early years, built in just three days in late May 1703. It is a small wooden cabin, with no foundations, heating stoves, or chimneys, in which Peter the Great lived only in the summer months.

In the two rooms of the cabin, built of pine logs painted to resemble bricks, there was only modest furniture and various tools hung on the walls (the czar was at journeyman—or master—level in 14 crafts).

When the Summer Palace was built Peter moved there, but his cabin was preserved as a monument to Saint Petersburg's history. It was opened as a museum in 1930. One of the star attractions in the museum is the rowing boat it is said was built by Peter himself.

THE STRELKA COMPLEX ON VASILEVSKIY ISLAND

Strelka: this is the name, which literally means "arrow," given in Saint Petersburg to the tongue of land at the far eastern tip of Vasilevskiy Island, the largest of the islands at the mouth of the Neva.

This point that divides the river into two arms (the Bolshaya [Great] Neva to the south and the Malaya [Small] Neva to the north), was the center of commerce in Saint Petersburg; from the 1730's until the 1880's the city's port was located here.

Here and on the facing page, views of the Strelka with the former Stock Exchange building and the Rostral Columns.

THE FORMER STOCK EXCHANGE

The central portion of the Strelka, Pushkin Square yesterday and Stock Exchange Square today, is overshadowed by the former Stock Exchange building illuminated by its white colonnade. This splendid example of Neoclassical architecture was built in 1805-1810 to plans by the Swiss T. de Thomon assisted by A. Zakharov.
The building, which recalls an ancient Greek temple, rests on a mighty granite base. A wide stairway, also in granite, leads from the semicircular plaza to the main facade decorated with the statuary group of **Neptune on a chariot drawn by sea horses** among statues symbolizing the Russian rivers **Neva** and **Volkhov**. On the opposite (western) side of the building are representations of the **goddess of navigation** and **Mercury**, patron of commerce, surrounded by **river nymphs**.
Today, the former Stock Exchange is the home of the **Central Russian State Naval Museum**, one of the

As we walk through the ancient capital of the czars we should not be surprised to make unusual acquaintances. In fact, it is the order of the day to meet friendly bears and figures in period costumes who evoke the splendor of the Imperial period, one and all ready to be photographed by curious tourists. A truly exceptional snapshot!

country's oldest; this museum was founded in 1709 by decree of Peter I, who in this manner assured preservation of his model ships. Among the exhibit pieces are paintings by famous artists, weapons, battle standards and ships' flags. Orders, medals, maps and charts of voyages to faraway places and naval expeditions, mementos unique in their genre, and documents of great historical value. There is also an **oaken boat**, found in the Yuzhny Bug river where it had lain for about three thousand years: it is a unique testimony of the ancient ties of the ancestors of the Slavs with their neighbors on the

The Strelka and Italy

The history and the art of Italy are not out of sight even on this tongue of land; it in fact seems that the Stock Exchange was modeled on one of the Greek temples at Paestum, probably that called the "Basilica." The Rostral Columns, instead, hark back to ancient Rome—in the 3rd and 2nd centuries BC there were raised in the Roman squares "rostral columns" ornamented with trophies: prows of Carthaginian ships symbolizing Rome's maritime victories over the North African capital.

coasts. And again, **Peter I's famous small-masted wooden vessel** from which the regular Russian fleet grew, and the personal effects of Peter I (the axe he used in the boatyards to build ships, his moose-hide tobacco pouch) and of Admiral Pavel Nakhimov. The most important portions of the exhibit are dedicated to the history of the Russian and Soviet fleets.

At the same time as the Stock Exchange, the **granite riverside embankment** was built on piles, with two accesses to the Neva ending in enormous granite spheres sculpted by Samson Sukhanov.

THE ROSTRAL COLUMNS

Two monumental rostral columns, 32 meters in height, rise at the sides of Stock Exchange Square. They are adorned with protruding **ships' prows** and figures of **Naiads**—and like the rostral columns of ancient Rome celebrated the victories of the Roman fleet so the Strelka columns recall the victories of the Russian fleet. At their feet stand impressive **statues** symbolizing Russia's fluvial communications routes: the **Dnieper, Volga, Volkhov, and Neva rivers**. These statues are also the work of Samson Sukhanov. The siting of the Rostral Columns and the Stock Exchange building are testimony to the fact that this was the ancient port and trade center of Saint Petersburg. The copper bowls atop the columns were filled with hemp oil that was lit at dusk and transformed the columns into gigantic lighthouses that guided the ships into port. And still, on festival days, the Rostral Columns burn with gas-fed flames.

On these pages, the monumental Rostral Columns and details of their decoration: ships' prows and allegorical statues of Russia's rivers.

THE CUSTOMS BUILDINGS AND THE ZOOLOGICAL MUSEUM

In the first years of the decade of the 1830's the Strelka architectural complex was completed with construction of the customs building and warehouse on the embankment of the Malaya Neva; work was directed by the architect Lucchini in obeisance to the general plan worked out by A. Zakharov.

The Customs House is adorned with a severe portico and the **statues of Mercury**, the god of trade, of **Neptune**, god of the seas, and of **Ceres** or Demeter, goddess of fertility. The dome of the Customs House was used as an observatory, from which were sent the signals announcing the arrival of ships in port. From 1927 on, the building hosted the Institute of Russian Literature and, later, also the **Literary Museum**.

The warehouse to the south (at University Embankment No. 1) is today the home of the **Zoological Museum**. Among the exhibits in this museum, one of the largest of its kind in the world, are unique collections of skeletons of animals and stuffed animals from both the prehistoric and modern eras. One of these is an embalmed mammoth that lived 44 million years ago and was discovered in the perpetually frozen wastes of Siberia in 1901. The collection of tropical butterflies and giant beetles is marvelous.

THE ACADEMY OF SCIENCES

In the late 18th century the old Kunstkammer building became too small for the Academy of Sciences; it was thus decided to build, between 1783 and 1789, a new building nearby. This so-called "main" building of the Academy of Sciences is a masterpiece by the architect Giacomo Quarenghi, replicating the noble forms of Classical style; it is decorated only with an impressive portico with eight columns, a pediment, and the double stairway that descends from the main entrance to the sidewalk.

MONUMENT TO MIKHAIL LOMONOSOV

Alongside the Academy of Sciences rises the monument to Mikhail Lomonosov, the great scholar of the 1700's, an authentic and widely-learned genius and the first Russian member of the Academy. The bronze statue, by V. Sveshnikov and B. Petrov, shows Lomonosov not in formal dress or with the traditional wig, but clad in simple work clothes.

On the facing page: the former Customs building with its soaring dome, and the Academy of Sciences, a masterpiece by Giacomo Quarenghi.

On these two pages: the Palace Bridge, the elegant Baroque building housing the Kunstkammer, and the Neo-Classical Academy of Sciences.

THE KUNSTKAMMER

Over the course of more than two centuries, one of the centers of Russian scientific thought formed on the Strelka. The role of the Kunstkammer (University Embankment No. 3) in this process was of primary importance. It was the first Russian natural history museum.

Peter I's private collections were full of curiosities: rare stones, fantastic embalmed animals, Buddhist idols, anatomical specimens . . . These collections later formed the nucleus of a public museum. Entrance was open to anyone and free of charge, and more often than not the visitors were offered a glass of vodka and a bite to eat. Since the Kunstkammer collections were crowded in the rooms of the Summer Palace, the current building, one of the city's oldest, was built especially to house them. It was erected in the years 1718-1734 by

the architects G. Mattarnovi, G. Chiaveri, N. Gherbel, and M. Zemtsov, and not without reason was nicknamed the "cradle of Russian science." This splendid example of early Baroque architecture consists of three three-story main buildings with two symmetrical wings connected by an elegant central tower.

Today, this ancient building houses the **Institute of Ethnography** named for the well-known Russian ethnographer and traveler Miklukho-Maklai, and two museums. The Kunstkammer collections were the foundation of the **Peter the Great Museum of Anthropology and Ethnography**, one of the world's most important. The exhibits in the **M. Lomonosov Museum** reflect the life and scientific work of the great Russian scholar: his scientific equipment, his astronomical instruments, his books, and an accurate model of his chemical laboratory, the first in all of Russia.

THE TWELVE COLLEGES

Beyond the *Mendeleevskaya Liniya* ("Mendeleev Line") boulevard there extends a gigantic building (about 400 meters in length), one of the largest of the city's old edifices, occupied by the **University of Saint Petersburg**.
In place of the innumerable state bodies called *prikaz*, in 1718 Czar Peter I created a number of "colleges" that became ministries in the early 19th century.

The architect Domenico Trezzini was charged with designing, for the twelve colleges, a building structured in such a manner as to express the independence of each college in all that regarded resolution of the problems of their individual competence and at the same time to stress the unitary nature of the tasks imposed on them by the state.
This building, composed of twelve identical linked sections, was raised in the years 1722-1741.

MENSHIKOV PALACE

At No. 15 University Embankment we see an interesting building designed for Prince Alexander Menshikov. The edifice, three stories in height with high mansards, was built in 1710-1714 by the architects G. Fontana and G. Schädel.
In 1981, the building was annexed to the Hermitage and became the home of the permanent exhibit entitled "**Russian Culture in the First Third of the Eighteenth Century.**"

The elegant Baroque building of the Twelve Colleges, designed by Domenico Trezzini. Bottom, the sumptuous Menshikov Palace.

The walls of the central atrium are painted in imitation marble and the niches host ancient statues. The wall-coverings of the rooms are magnificent, with white Dutch tiles with cobalt-blue decorations: the majority of the scenes are pastoral, with at least 120 different subjects. The interiors of the palace are adorned with 25 thousand ceramic tiles; 1500 of these were created by the Saint Petersburg restorers who succeeded in understanding the secrets of the Dutch masters.

Menshikov's favorite room was the **Walnut Study**, clad in panels of Persian walnut. The walls were adorned with the **portrait of Peter I** painted in Amsterdam, whence Menshikov had accompanied Peter I as his aide and treasurer, and the **amber-framed mirror** given to Peter in 1709 by the king of Prussia.

Other beautiful pieces are the **camp clock** with its walnut case, made in England in the early 18th century, the **carved and gilded chairs** made in Italy, again in the early 18th century, and the small table with its **amber chess set**: Menshikov was an aficionado of the game.

The Walnut Study in the Menshikov Palace, the obelisk raised in honor of the Russian leader Rumyantsev, and the Academy of Arts, a shining example of the transition from the Baroque to Neo-Classicism.

THE ACADEMY OF ARTS

The Academy of Arts building (University Embankment No. 17) was raised in 1764-1788 by the architects A. Kokorinov and J. Vallin de la Mothe. The major facade, on the embankment, is more solemn than the others. Its center is placed in evidence by a portico of columns on which rests a triangular pediment. The center entrance is surmounted by the **statues of Hercules and Flora**.

This building is one of the most eloquent expressions of the transition from the Baroque to the Neo-Classical in Russian architecture. The center staircase and the atrium of the main entrance are important architectural works. In the years 1832-1834, in front of the main facade of the academy, there was built a rigorously Classical stairway designed by K. Ton and adorned with **two Egyptian sphinxes** on high bases. and granite benches with griffins and bronze "windmill" streetlamps. Russia purchased the sphinxes from Egypt in 1831.

The garden alongside the Academy now hosts an **obelisk to General Rumyantsev**, who more than once won out over the Turks; it originally stood in the Field of Mars.

The Hermitage

*T*his one of the world's most famous and largest museums and its vast collections occupy the most beautiful and majestic complex of buildings in the entire city: the **Winter Palace**, the **Small Hermitage** (the original private museum of Catherine II), the **Old Hermitage**, the **Hermitage Theater**, and the **New Hermitage** (the first public museum).

In the last few years this historical "nucleus" has been flanked by the Menshikov Palace, the General Staff Building, and the building adjacent to the Theater. The Hermitage collections were first opened to the public in 1852, and were at the time called the "Imperial Museum": today's official denomination is "State Hermitage Museum."

The Winter Palace in Numbers

The Winter Palace is striking in terms not only of beauty but also of sheer size. It is more than 200 meters long, 200 in width, 22 in height, while the overall length of the cornice that runs around the building is about 2 kilometers. The palace contains 1057 rooms on a surface area of 46,516 square meters, 117 staircases, 1786 doors, 1945 windows, and 176 statues on the eaves of the roof. For a long time the Winter Palace was the city's tallest building. In 1844, Nicholas I issued an ordinance stating that private homes had to be at least one *sagen* (about 2 meters) lower than the Winter Palace; this rule remained in force until 1905.

THE WINTER PALACE

This oldest construction in the Hermitage complex was built in 1754-1762 to plans by the architect Francesco Bartolomeo Rastrelli. Despite its gigantic size, the first thing we notice about the palace is its graciousness rather than its mass. This admirable work in Russian Baroque style harmoniously alternates outcroppings and recesses in the architecture and is characterized by its many columns with a purely decorative function and the richness of its sculptural ornamentation. The grilles, the

Francesco Bartolomeo Rastrelli.

The Winter Palace, a splendid and harmonious synthesis of might and grace, with the north facade on the Palace Embankment and the west looking toward the Admiralty.

gates, the portals, and the balustrades of the gala entrances to the palace all draw complicated arabesques. The rooms in the interior form interminable fugues of spaces.

Rastrelli gave an original touch to each single facade of the Winter Palace, the city's largest and most elegant building. The pronounced wings of the west facade (toward the Admiralty) delimited the Court of Honor. The north facade, facing the Neva, was built by Rastrelli in more sober forms: the white columns arranged in two loggias create a wonderful play of light and shadow. The main facade, running along Palace Square, is broken by the three arches of the entrances. The pea green color of the walls contrasts favorably with the splendor of the columns. The decoration of the building is reinforced by the sinuosity of the complicated cornices and by the innumerable ornamental *friezes* of the windows including heads of cherubs, leonine masks, and bizarre curlicues. The *statues* above the cornice of the roof, alternating with *vases*, make the profile of the palace all that more interesting and exalt the dynamics of its forms. The architecture and the astounding beauty of the interiors of the Winter Palace are in and of themselves jewels of incalculable value. But for mankind, the fact that this incredible palace is the main building of the Hermitage Museum can only increase its already inestimable worth.

History

In times past, five buildings were known by the name of "Winter Palace." The first of these was *Peter I's Winter Palace* on the waterway known as the Winter Canal.
The *second Winter Palace* also stood on this canal; the main facade, however, overlooked the Neva. And here, in January 1725, Peter I died. In 1726-1727 this second Winter Palace was enlarged, redecorated, and improved to plans by Domenico Trezzini (and was thus the *third Winter Palace*).
In the decade of the 1730's, by order of the czarina Anna Ivanovna and based on the plans by F. B. Rastrelli, the *fourth Winter Palace* was built, restructuring the palace of Prince Apraksin that rose on the area occupied by today's Winter Palace. Peter I's daughter, the czarina Elizabeth Petrovna, ordered construction of a new Winter Palace, the *fifth*, for herself. And Rastrelli built a sumptuous wooden edifice along the Nevskiy Boulevard (today's Nevskiy Prospekt) that occupied the vast space between the Moyka river and what is today Malaya Morskaya Street. Elizabeth moved in with her servants and her incredible array of well-loved cats (more than one hundred!). But Elizabeth also ordered that Rastrelli build a *sixth Winter Palace*; the architect responded enthusiastically to the idea and wrote, "The Winter Palace will be built in masonry for the glory of Russia."

The building was the imperial residence until World War I, and in the summer of 1917 it became the headquarters of the provisional government. In October of the same year, the Winter Palace was proclaimed a national museum, on the same footing as the Hermitage.

The Optical Telegraph Turret

The roof of the Winter Palace sports a hexagonal turret, clearly not in Rastrelli's style. It was built in about 1830 to house the "optical telegraph" by means of which, in the period 1833-1854, the occupants of the Winter Palace kept in permanent contact with Tsarskoe Selo (the "Czar's Village"), with Gatchina, and even with the cities of Vilnus and Warsaw. Fixed to the wall of the turret facing the tower of the city Duma on the Nevskiy Prospekt (the second transmitter/receiver station of the optical telegraph) there was a T-shaped metal structure turning on a pin. Communications were effectuated by means of a signal alphabet: the various positions of the revolving "T" each corresponded to a letter of the alphabet. At dusk, the ends of the metal "T" were lighted. The signals were retransmitted by other towers, at heights of up to 17 meters; there were 149 transmitter/receiver stations of this type between Saint Petersburg and Warsaw.

Details of the facades of the Winter Palace. In particular, below and on the facing page, the optical telegraph turret and Saltykov's entranceway on the west facade, facing the Admiralty.

The central portion of the facade facing on Palace Square and a detail of one of the beautiful gates that give access to the inner courtyard and the Hermitage Museum.

The Entranceway

The Winter Palace is more than ever a destination for visitors: it is not a rare to see, along the sides of Palace Square, a queue of tourists awaiting the chance to pass through the elegant **gates** of the three arches of the main entrance. Once past these true works of art surmounted by the Imperial emblem, the visitor finds himself in the inner courtyard of the Palace, and from here, through the beautiful garden with its trees and benches under the inner facades of the Palace, as sumptuous as the exterior facades, the visitor enters the Hermitage Museum proper.

A Singular Triumphal Entry

Rastrelli's palace was ready, but the sudden death of Elizabeth meant it could not be inaugurated in style. The czarina's successor, Peter III, would have moved into the new residence immediately, but Palace Square was still encumbered by worksite debris: piles of bricks, planks, barrels of lime, beams. The triumphal entrance of the new czar into the sixth Winter Palace seemed a practical impossibility, but the chief of police came up with a solution: a proclamation stating that the lower middle classes could take anything they wanted from the square. A. Bolotov wrote in his memoirs that nigh onto the entire population of Saint Petersburg, with wheelbarrows, wagons, and even sleighs (despite the mild weather: it was Eastertide) poured into the square. Saint Petersburg's citizens took whatever they could: planks, bricks, clay, lime . . . and the square filled with clouds of dust. By evening, the area was completely cleared—and there was no longer any obstacle to Peter III's solemn accession to the new Winter Palace.

Details of the facades on the inner courtyard and the garden.

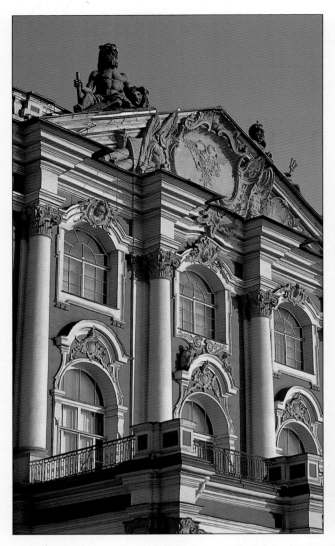

THE SMALL HERMITAGE

Construction of the Small Hermitage was ordered by Catherine II (Catherine the Great), who intended to isolate herself from the Winter Palace. The two-story building in Neoclassical style was built by Yuriy Velten and J. Vallin de la Mothe in 1764-67; it is composed of two main buildings with facades on the Palace Square and on the Neva, united by a hanging garden. Here, the empress began her private art collection, first purchasing 225 paintings from a Berlin antique dealer and later adding other art. In practice, this private museum became the first nucleus of the enormous museum we see today.

THE NEW HERMITAGE

Alongside the Small Hermitage, on Millionaires' Street, stands the New Hermitage building constructed in 1842-1851 to plans by Leo von Klenze, in collaboration with V. Stasov and N. Efimov, by order of Czar Nicholas I. This was the first building ever raised in Russia as a public museum. The entrance portico is decorated with ten gigantic *atlantes* in grey granite, sculpted to designs by A. Terebenev. The portico looks out on the stupendous panorama of Palace Square.

The facade of the Small Hermitage and, bottom, that of the New Hermitage on Millionaires' Street, with its portico supported by gigantic atlantes.
On the facing page, a view of the Winter Palace from the portico of the New Hermitage, with the atlantes in the foreground.

The interior of the Hermitage Theater, and, bottom, the line of the facades of the palaces that make up the complex on the Neva Embankment, with in the foreground a corner of the Winter Palace.

THE OLD HERMITAGE AND THE HERMITAGE THEATER

In 1787, again to plans by Velten and by order of Catherine II, another Neo-classical building was raised alongside the Neva to house the increasingly numerous art collections: and thus the Old Hermitage was born.

At the corner between the Palace Embankment and the Winter Canal, facing the Old Hermitage building, is the Hermitage Theater, construction of which was concluded in 1787 to plans by G. Quarenghi.

Taking as his model the theaters of antiquity and enacting Catherine's suggestions ("all the seats in this theater must be equally prestigious!"), the architect built the house in the form of an amphitheater—there are no boxes, galleries, or a real orchestra—with seats degrading toward the stage like wide steps.

The house is exceptionally beautiful, with its walls in yellow-red artificial marble. In the spaces between the columns are niches housing statues of Apollo and the nine Muses, while the spaces above the niches host the busts and medallions of Molière, Racine, Voltaire, and other dramatists and exponents of the dramatic arts. The Hermitage Theater was, in fact, the personal theater of Catherine II and her descendents.

After a period in which it was used as a conference hall for the Hermitage State Museum body, the theater has today returned to its original function.

The Hermitage Theater is linked to the Old Hermitage building by a gallery spanning the **Winter Canal**. From underneath the arches formed by this raised corridor the visitor to the complex can admire the poetic vision of the Neva and the soaring tower of the Peter and Paul Fortress.

The gallery over the Winter Canal from Millionaires' Street and, bottom, from the Neva, with the Hermitage Theater building on the left and the Old Hermitage on the right.

THE HERMITAGE MUSEUM

The Hermitage, today known worldwide, was given its name by Catherine II. It contains collections of works of art unique in their genres; traditionally, the date of foundation of the Hermitage is considered as being 1764, when Catherine's collection of 225 paintings purchased in Berlin was transferred to the Winter Palace. The collection grew rapidly: by 1774 it already counted 2080 paintings and numerous drawings, precious stones, sculptures, and artistic crafts works. Today, the Hermitage is the State treasure-house of works of art: it owns 2,700,000 items (paintings, sculptures, drawings, engravings, rare furniture, jewels, historical costumes, coins, medals, weapons, and household and other items), all of inestimable value and thanks to which we can study the development of all aspects of world culture from ancient time to ours.

The Main Staircase of the Winter Palace

In 1837, the sumptuous main staircase (Jordan Staircase) of the Winter Palace was damaged by fire, and during the work for restoring this entrance the architect Vasiliy Stasov made some modifications to its original design, drafted by the architect Francesco Bartolomeo Rastrelli. The magnificence of the staircase is disarming: splendid the gilded stuccowork adorning the walls, blinding the white marble of the statues, impressive the gigantic ceiling painted with representations featuring the gods of Olympus.

Opening off the upper landing of the staircase is the **Field Marshals' Hall** (so-called because here were hung the portraits of the Russian field marshals). From here, corridors with walls lined with tapestries lead to the adjacent Winter Palace or to the Small Hermitage.

The main staircase and a detail of the Winter Palace's Pavilion Hall. Top, a 6th-century BC Greek cup.

Pavilion Hall

Pavilion Hall in the Small Hermitage was created to designs by Andrei Stakenschneider in 1856. The hall is a concentrate of eclecticism where the most disparate styles cohabit: from elements of Mauritanian art to the architecture of the Renaissance and of antiquity. Nevertheless, the architect's skill succeeded in harmonizing the various heterogeneous elements that contribute to the decoration of the hall. The colors of Pavilion Hall are light and festive; the slender white marble columns support an elegant gallery and the crystal of 28 chandeliers reverberates throughout.

The admirable mosaic that adorns the hall's floor was created in 1847-1851 in Saint Petersburg, and in one-half scale reproduces the mosaic discovered in 1780 during excavation of the Roman baths of Emperor Titus. The windows on the north side of Pavilion Hall open on the Neva, in direction of the Peter and Paul Fortress, while the southern windows afford a view of the hanging garden created atop the ground-floor vaults. Pavilion Hall also contains an original object in a glass case: the celebrated **Peacock Clock**, made in London by the famous goldsmith and jeweler James Cox. It was a gift from Prince Grigoriy Potemkin to the czarina Catherine II.

Top, a silver amphora (4th century BC) from the Scythian tumulus at Certomlyk. The "Great Room" and, on the next page, the "Raphael Loggias" built by G. Quarenghi and frescoed by H. Unterberger in the late 18th century, copying the originals in the Vatican.

The Soviet Staircase

This staircase was called by this name even before the Revolution: it was used by court dignitaries and members of the State Council (the term "soviet" means "council"), when they came from the Winter Palace to take part in the meetings presided over by the emperor. The Soviet or Council Staircase connects three buildings: a corridor leads to the Small Hermitage, on the opposite side rises the Old Hermitage (on the second floor of which is the exhibit of Italian art), and the center doors (across from the windows) lead to the rooms housing the collections of Dutch art (in the New Hermitage building).

The Twenty Columns Hall

The Twenty Columns Hall is the home of the exhibit of **Italian vases**. The floor of this hall is a mosaic made of some hundreds of thousands of fragments of stone. Further ahead is one of the most beautiful works by the Russian masters of the chisel: the famous **Kolyvanskaya vase**. This gigantic vase cannot be moved, since it is too large to pass through the doors; in fact, it was set here before the outer wall was built. The vase is more than 2.5 meters in height; the greatest diameter of the bowl is about 5 meters and the lower portion more than 3 meters. The bowl weighs 19 tons: the world's heaviest vase!

Art and Culture in the Ancient World

The best of the items that make up this collection—objects in gold and other precious materials dating from the 5th century BC to the 3rd century AD—are found in the **Hermitage's Gold Collection** "treasure rooms."

This area contains magnificent gold and silverware of the Scythian and Samartian civilizations as well as western European jewelry from the 16th to the 19th centuries.

The statues are especially lovely: in particular the **bust of the Roman emperor** Marcus Julius Severus Philippus, called the Arab (3rd-century AD), who usurped his predecessor to assume power in Rome, and the magnificent statue of the **Tauride Venus** (Aphrodite) dating to the 3rd century BC. This sculpture, which represents the goddess of love and beauty, was called thus because it came from the palace in Tauris where it had been kept for a long time.

Our visit to the culture and **art of ancient Greece** obviously extends to the collection, unique in the world, of Attic red-figured vases. Of particular interest among these is the pelike known as the "**Swallow Vase**," a work of inestimable value by Euphronius dating to the 6th century BC; then there is the collection of the elegant statuettes in terracotta produced in **Tanagra** in the 4th and 3rd centuries BC.

The collection of sculpted stone (Catherine II purchased 10,000 items of this type over 10 years) counts one of the Hermitage's most famous masterpieces, the famous **Gonzaga cameo**, a 3rd-century BC work from Alexandria. It is a small slab with three layers of sardonyx, a configuration that allowed the cutter to obtain splendid effects of light and shadow. The cameo carries two portraits: that of the Egyptian king Ptolemy II Philadelphus and of his wife Arsinoe.

Italian Art in the 13th to 18th Centuries

This section contains works by the most important Italian artists from **Simone Martini** to **Beato Angelico**, from **Leonardo da Vinci** to **Michelangelo**, and from **Raphael** to **Titian**; and again, **Giorgione**, **Caravaggio**, **Canova**, and others.

The museum is home to two canvases by Leonardo da Vinci: the **Madonna with a Flower** (or the **Benois Madonna**, from the name of its former owner), an early work by the great master, and the celebrated **Litta Madonna**, painted in about 1490 and purchased by the Marchese di Litta. Two in number are also the canvases by Raphael: the **Conestabile Madonna**, which he painted at only eighteen years of age (a small painting that expresses a profound lyricism), and a **Holy Family**.

The only work by Michelangelo in any Russian collection is the **Crouching Boy**. The statue was intended for the tomb of the Medici family, the rulers of Florence, but it remained unused for that purpose.

The maximum exponent of the Venetian school of painting, Titian, is represented at the Hermitage by only eight

The well-known Gonzaga Cameo, with the portraits of Arsinoe and Ptolemy II Philadelphus (3rd century BC) and the equally-famous Danae *by Titian (1546-1553).*

canvases: among these, **The Repentant Magdalene**. Titian did not adhere to the legend of the repentant sinner who escaped into the desert; he instead painted a stupendous Venetian woman overcome by strong emotion, with flowing golden tresses, tumid lips, and eyes overflowing with tears. The "agitated" landscape that forms the background to the image underlines the deep unrest that torments Magdalene.

In his painting of **Saint Sebastian**, Titian shows the Christian saint pierced by the arrows of the Romans. Death is inevitable, but the spirit of Saint Sebastian is not swayed. The pictorial technique used in this canvas reveals how the artist applied his colors with rapid brushstrokes—and even with his hands and fingers.

Spanish Art (15th Century to early 19th Century)

The art of Spain is represented from the 15th century through the early 19th. The Hermitage contains works by such great masters as **El Greco**, **Ribera**, **Zurbarán**, **Velázquez**, **Murillo**, and **Goya**.

The **Cavaliers' Hall** exhibits western European armor and weapons of war, tournament instruments, and hunting weapons.

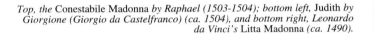

Top, the Conestabile Madonna *by Raphael (1503-1504); bottom left,* Judith *by Giorgione (Giorgio da Castelfranco) (ca. 1504), and bottom right, Leonardo da Vinci's* Litta Madonna *(ca. 1490).*

The Flemish, Dutch, and German Masters

Among the Flemish masters stand out the figures of *Van Dyck*, the eminent portraitist, and *Peter Paul Rubens*.

Van Dyck's *Self Portrait* represents the master with little respect for convention: the somewhat listless, well-tended hands and the languid gaze underline the author's artistic nature. Among the more than 40 works by Rubens are *The Union of Earth and Water*, a canvas that allegorically recalled to the Flemish the need for Flanders to find an access to the sea without which prosperity in their country was an impossibility. In this work, as in the majority of his other canvases, Rubens glorifies wealth, abundance and the sense of gioie-de-vivre.

Another celebrated painting by Rubens is *Infanta's Maid*: the idealized image of his daughter Clara who died in 1623, two years before Rubens painted the portrait.

The 26 canvases by the Dutch master *Rembrandt* are one of the Hermitage's greatest prides. One of his best works is undoubtedly the *Return of the Prodigal Son*. This work touches us with its great humanity: in the great dark space that is the canvas the only points of light are the face of the father who lost his sight during the long years of awaiting his son, the old man's hands, and the figure of the prodigal son kneeling at the feet of his father; the painting admirably expresses the tragedy of a man who vainly wasted his life due to irresponsibility but at the same time it is an exhortation to aid those who have fallen into misfortune.

True jewels in the German collection are the works by *Lucas Cranach the Elder*, whose eclectic talent is exemplified at the Hermitage by works like *Venus and Cupid*, the *Portrait of a Woman in a Hat*, and the *Virgin and Child Beneath an Apple Tree*.

15th-20th Century French Painting

The French artists are also very well-represented at the Hermitage; worthy of special mention are **Louis Le Nain**, **Claude Lorrain**, **Nicolas Poussin**, and again **Antoine Watteau**, **Jean Honoré Fragonard**, **Etienne-Maurice Falconet**, and **Jean-Antoine Houdon**. One of Louis Le Nain's best works is on exhibit: **The Dairymaid's Family**. The aspect of the figures in the painting belies indigence and the difficulty of living a hard life; nonetheless the features of these peasants are illuminated with a sense of great dignity.

The works by Nicolas Poussin testify to the appearance in France of a new current, Classicism, affirmation of civic ideals and aspiration to the creative capacity of reason. One of Poussin's finest works is **Tancredi and Erminia**. This canvas renders the episode from Torquato Tasso's poem *Jerusalem Delivered* in which the

Top:
Infanta's Maid
(ca. 1625)
by Peter Paul Rubens.

Center:
Return of the Prodigal Son
(1668-1669)
by Rembrandt.

Capricious Lady *(ca. 1718)*
by Jean-Antoine Watteau.

Bottom:
Woman in a Garden *(1867)*
by Claude Monet.

heroine cuts her hair to bind Tancredi's wounds. In the same room hangs the other painting by Poussin, **Landscape with Polyphemus**: here, the painter gives concrete form to his dream of a harmonious world based on reason. The Cyclops Polyphemus, after having enchanted the river nymphs with the notes of his flute, climbs to the top of the mountain, almost unrecognizable among the features of the landscape. The sounds of the flute seem to announce the reign of that beauty and harmony that dominate nature. Jean-Antoine Watteau, son of a humble mason, became one of France's major painters. To the artificial and static figures of the academic canvases, he counterposed images of real people expressing all the features of their individual characters; a shining example is the **Capricious Lady**, in which a woman turns her back to a petulant cavalier while her face expresses determination and aloofness.

Among the various sculptural works we must mention **Voltaire**, a work by Jean-Antoine Houdon that renders the seated figure of the distinguished French thinker and writer with great expressiveness, underlining the audacity of his mind and that love for life before which even senility is forced to lay down its arms.

If the visitor must limit himself to a single visit to the

On the facing page: (top) Boulevard Montmartre on a Sunny Afternoon *(1897) by Camille Pissarro,* Woman with a Fruit *(1893) by Paul Gauguin, and* The Absinthe Drinker *(1901) by Pablo Picasso.*

Portrait of the Actress Jeanne Samary *(1878) by Auguste Renoir,* Place de la Trinity in Paris *(1910) by Albert Marquet, and* Voltaire (1781) by Jean-Antoine Houdon.

Woman in Blue *(late 1770's) by Thomas Gainsborough and* Eternal Spring *(after 1884), a sculpture by Auguste Rodin.*

by the self-taught mechanic Ivan Kulibin, who presented it to Catherine II. This clock does not only mark time: every 15 minutes it emits musical sounds and at noon plays a motif taken from a cantata composed by Kulibin himself in honor of Catherine II. What is more, at every top of the hour a small door opens to reveal a chamber in which tiny figures in gold and silver recite the scene of the "Resurrection of Christ."

This section is also home to the *mosaics* made under the guidance of the leading Russian scientist and artist Mikhail Lomonosov, and the *portrait of Peter I* created personally by Lomonosov.

Hermitage, not to be missed are the paintings by *E. Delacroix*, *J. Millet*, and *C. Corot*.

In the decade of the 1870's, France saw the affirmation of the group known as the Impressionists, among whose principal exponents were *Claude Monet*, *Edgar Degas*, and *Pierre-Auguste Renoir*. The exhibit includes Monet's famous painting of the *Woman in a Garden,* Renoir's marvelous *Portrait of the Actress Jeanne Samary*, and canvases by *Paul Cézanne*, *Paul Gauguin*, *Henri Matisse* (with the feted *Danse*), and *Pablo Picasso* as well as sculptures by *Auguste Rodin* and other great masters of French art.

English Painting in the 17th-19th Centuries

The collections of the English school of painting in the 17th to 19th centuries are dominated by portraits and landscapes: of especial interest are the works of the great painters *Joshua Reynolds* and *Thomas Gainsborough*.

Russian Art and Culture

The section on Russian art and culture is a particularly interesting one. Here we can admire works of artistic craftsmanship like, for example, the *vase carved from a walrus tusk* in 1798 by the master craftsman Nikolai Vereshchagin of the Arkhangelsk region. This vase, which resembles a delicate embroidery, is topped by a tiny replica of the monument to Peter I on the Neva river embankment.

Another outstanding piece is the famous *clock* in the form (and the size) of a goose-egg: it was built in 1769

The Peacock Clock

The Peacock Clock is a quite complex work. The central figure is a large peacock set on a tall oaken log with two branches, from one of which hangs a braid of silver cords supporting a cage surrounded by little bells. Inside the cage is an owl in burnished silver, underneath a squirrel intent on nibbling walnuts. A life-sized multicolored rooster also roosts on the log. The list of inhabitants of the glass case includes snails, lizards, and crickets among mushrooms, leaves, and acorns. Drawn on the cap of the largest mushroom is the face of the clock: when it is wound up, all the figures move in turn: the first is the owl, who turns its head, moves its eyes, and scratches with its foot. At the same time the cage turns and the bells tinkle delicately and melodically. When the music ceases the peacock's tail opens and the bird turns slowly, showing off its beautiful plumage and nodding its head graciously. Then the rooster awakens, stretches its neck, opens its beak, and crows. On the clock face on the mushroom, the hours are shown in Roman numerals, the minutes in Arabic notation, and the cricket that jumps on the mushroom counts the seconds.

The Malachite Room

The Malachite Room, with its windows over the Neva, is literally dumbfounding. The room takes its name from the fact that the columns, pillars, and fireplaces are all clad in decorative slabs of precious malachite. The green of the stone is an original accompaniment to the gilded stuccowork of the ceiling and doors, the white of the walls, and the crimson silk of the upholstery of the furniture. The room hosts a great quantity of objects, also in malachite (vases, coffers, etc.). Our attention is inexorably drawn to a display case called the "Tropical Forest" in which the palm fronds, the feathers of the birds, and the flower petals are all in tiny chips of malachite in various tonalities.

In a nearby room is exhibited the *sarcophagus of Alexander Nevsky*, made in 1750-1753 in the Mint that is still operating in the Peter and Paul Fortress. About a ton and a half of silver was used in its construction. The tall sarcophagus is decorated with

scenes from the life of Alexander Nevsky and is surmounted by a pyramid decorated with the monogram and portrait of the prince.

Another room contains sculptures by **Bartolomeo Carlo Rastrelli** (the architect Rastrelli's father): the bronze busts of **Peter I** and his faithful companion **Alexander Menshikov**. In these busts, the sculptor laudably rendered the intelligence, the will power, and the determination that characterized Peter the Great.

Peter the Great's Hall

Following the visit to these collections, and before leaving the Winter Palace, it is worthwhile to stop for awhile in Peter the Great's Hall or Small Throne Room alongside the Field Marshal's Hall mentioned above. The vaults are decorated with gilded arabesques and on the side walls hang two canvases representing scenes of battle during the Great Northern War. At the far end of the room is the official portrait of *Peter I with the allegorical figure of Glory* (1730) by the Venetian painter J. Amigoni. The **throne** in front of the painting was built in 1731 by the English crafts master N. Clausen in ebonized oak and gilded silver.

We now pass through the adjacent *Hall of the State Seal* (this hall was used for formal receptions) and enter the famed *Military Gallery* in which are exhibited **332 portraits** of the most famous combatants of the wars fought by Russia against Napoleon's armies. Almost all the portraits were painted in the decade of the 1820's by the painters **G. Dawe, A. Polyakov**, and **V. Golike**.

Top, malachite vase (1840's).

The Malachite Room in the Winter Palace and the bronze bust of Peter I (1723) by Bartolomeo Carlo Rastrelli.

The Military Gallery in the Winter Palace and two artistic vases on exhibit at the museum.

On the facing page, Peter the Great's Hall (or Small Throne Room).

The Hall of Saint George or the Great Throne Room

Our visit to the collections and the rooms of the Hermitage concludes in the **Hall of Saint George** (or **Great Throne Room**), with its 800 square meters extension. The elegant stands of 48 paired marble columns support a balcony that runs around the hall, interrupted only at the center of the far wall, where above the current site of the throne is a huge relief of **Saint George and the Dragon**. Another stupendous feature of this hall is the parquet, made of 16 different rare woods. The parquet repeats the ceiling arabesques as though in a mirror, so enhancing the artistic harmony of this enormous hall.

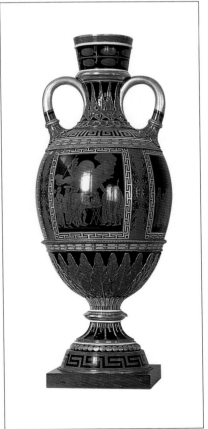

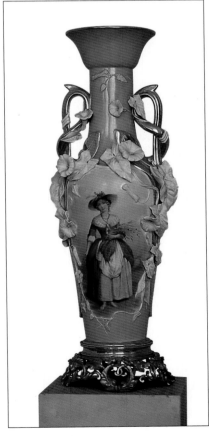

PALACE SQUARE

*I*n essence, Palace Square is delimited by the gigantic arcaded **General Staff Building**, an appreciable model of Classicism, and the southern facade of the **Winter Palace**, a masterpiece of the Baroque. At first sight it may seem that buildings in such different architectural styles would not harmonize well; instead, this extraordinary square, together with the **Guards' Headquarters** building and the **Alexander Column**, give the impression of a harmonious architectural complex. It is not to be excluded that a major factor in creating this impression is the uniformity of the horizontal development of the buildings that line the square, one of the largest in Saint Petersburg (59,964 square meters).

The square with the General Staff Building, the Alexander Column, and the Monumental Arch.
Characters in 18th-century costume and shays are an open invitation to a souvenir photo or a ride around the city.

THE GENERAL STAFF BUILDING

With the aim of lending to the city's main square a unitary architectural look, in the early 19th century the government commandeered all the private buildings that abutted the square on the south side and in 1819 the architect Carlo Rossi was ordered to reconstruct them as the headquarters for the Russian army. In accordance with the plans drafted by the architect, two grandiose Neoclassical buildings were raised. Their facades extend for a length of about 580 meters (a record in Europe).

The facades are slightly concave and set out in such a manner as to form an enormous open semicircle opening onto the Winter Palace; they are linked by a grandiose arch of triumph symbolizing the victory of the Russian forces over Napoleon's armies. The works for construction of the palace were concluded in 1829. Today, the western wing hosts various **exhibit spaces** of the Hermitage Museum.

THE CENTRAL SQUARES COMPLEX

7 he three most central of the city's squares are **Palace Square** (which we have already seen), **Decembrists' Square**, and **Saint Isaac's Square**. The major monuments are the **Winter** **Palace**, the **General Staff Building**, the **Admiralty**, and **Saint Isaac's Cathedral**, not to mention the other architectural masterpieces—all of which contribute to forming a single complex of varying volumes on the left bank of the Neva.

The "Bronze Horseman" in Decembrists' Square, with the Neo-Classical Senate and Synod buildings in the background.

DECEMBRISTS' SQUARE

This was formerly Senate Square, on the west side of the Admiralty. It was given its current name in 1925 in memory of the Russian nobles who in December 1825 were the first in the history of the country to rise, armed, against czarist rule and the feudal regime. To the east, the square is delimited by splendid Neoclassical buildings: the **Senate** (at the corner on the Neva) and the **Holy Synod**, joined by a **triumphal arch** (all works by Carlo Rossi), and the **Horse Guard's Riding School**, by Giacomo Quarenghi.

The "Bronze Horseman"
Decembrists' Square is also the site of the famous monument to Czar Peter I by the French sculptor Etienne Falconet, who with this work attempted to express the French Encyclopaedists' idea of "illuminated absolutism" (the monarch who leads his country toward progress: the ladder symbolizes overcoming difficulties; the crushed serpent the victory of good over evil). Peter I, crowned with laurel, has stopped his careering horse and forced it to submit to his unyielding will. The granite pedestal is carved with the laconic inscription in Russian and Latin characters: "To Peter I – Catherine II." The date, 1782, is that of the inauguration of the monument: the hundredth anniversary of Peter I's ascent to the throne. The monument inspired Pushkin' poem "The Bronze Horseman"; hence the name by which it is best known.

THE ADMIRALTY

Built in 1806-1823 by the architect Andrei Zakharov on the site of two earlier buildings dating to 1705 and 1730, the Admiralty is an imposing construction.

The main facade, 407 meters in width, is broken by porticoes with six and twelve columns. Zakharov also preserved the U-shaped plan of the earlier building and the old slender spire, surmounted by the gilded form of the caravel that dominates the city from its 72.5 meters' height. Despite the fact that it weighs 65 kilograms, the caravel turns freely in its mounting to indicate the direction of the wind.

The heightened spire that tops the building is the fulcrum of the system of adjacent squares and the three arteries that radiate out from it (the famed Nevskiy Prospekt, Gorokhovaya Street, and the Voznesenskiy Prospekt).

Ships were built in the Admiralty shipyards until 1844; in 1870, the area of the plaza looking toward the Neva was built up. Until 1917 the Admiralty buildings were the headquarters of the Ministry of the Navy.

The Statues and Reliefs

The *high relief* above the main entrance to the Admiralty was inspired by Czar Peter I's creation of the Russian fleet: the sea-god Neptune presents to the czar his trident, symbol of the dominion of the seas. Alongside Peter, the goddess of wisdom Minerva —impersonated by a young woman seated under a laurel bush—addresses Russia. Russia rests against Hercules' club (symbol of might) and holds the cornucopia near which is Mercury, god of trade, on sacks of goods.

Above this high relief, at the corners of the lower cube of the Admiralty tower, stand the statues of the great commanders and heroes of antiquity: Achilles, Ajax, Pyrrhus, and Alexander the Great.

The colonnade of the upper cube of the tower is decorated with *28 statues* (the same number as the columns), representing the four ele-

The artistic main facade of the Admiralty with the monumental entrance overlooked by the elegant tower and spire.

ments of nature (Fire, Water, Air, and Earth), the four seasons, and the four winds was well as the mythological protectors of shipbuilders and astronomers, the goddesses Isis and Urania.

At the sides of the arch at the main entrance are two **monumental groups** each eleven meters in height. Each of these compositions, representing three nymphs, symbolizes one aspect of the goddess Hecate of mythology, who in her three aspects impersonated Water, Earth, and the Heavens.

The pediments of the side porticoes are adorned with **high reliefs**: the blindfolded Fortune crowning Industry (right of the tower), Fortune distributing awards for military and maritime valor (left of the tower), Glory crowning military valor (on the Decembrists' Square side), and Glory crowning Science (on the Palace Square side). The artists F. Scedrin, S. Pimenov, I. Terebenev, and V. Demut-Malinovskiy all contributed to the sculptural enrichment of the Admiralty.

Alexander II Park

The gardens running along the walls of the Admiralty were created on occasion of the bicentennial celebrations of the birth of Peter I. But Alexander II, who certainly did not suffer from false modesty, had it given his name. In the park, which extends over a vast area even into a portion of the former Senate Square, are **monuments** to the **writers V. Zhukovskiy**, **N. Gogol**, and **M. Lermontov**, to the composer **M. Glinka**, and to the famous explorer **Nikolai Przhevalskiy**, an eminent geographer and the first explorer of central Asia, who in 9 years and 3 months traveled 32,000 kilometers through uncharted lands.

Details of the tower and the arch at the entrance to the Admiralty, adorned with statues and allegorical reliefs, and the Alexander II Park.

On these pages, images of Saint Isaac's Cathedral, the city's most magnificent, and of the sculptures on the exterior.

On pages 66-67, a view of the interior of the church with the precious iconostasis and the mosaic of Saint Peter.

SAINT ISAAC'S CATHEDRAL

The building that today dominates the square of the same name, the fifth in chronological order, was begun in 1817 by the French architect Montferrand who until that time was an illustrious unknown. Today, the church is a *museum*.

The great building, with its solemn *porticoes and colonnades*, with its marvelous *bronze sculptures* and the famous *gilded dome*, took forty years to build.

The southern pediment is adorned with a high relief of the *Adoration of the Magi* by Ivan Vitali. By the same sculptor, the high relief above the west portico portraying the *Saint Isaac the Dalmatian meeting Emperor Theodosius*, symbolizing the union of temporal and spiritual power; beside Theodosius is his wife Flaccilla (the two figures are portrayed in the guises of Nicholas I and his wife). In the left corner of the relief is Auguste de Montferrand holding a model of the church. Above the north portico, the *Resurrection of Christ*, on the east pediment *Saint Isaac Meeting Emperor Valens*. Over each pediment are figures of the *Evangelists*. The sumptuous interior is rich in works of art. Of note the ceiling of the dome with the splendid fresco of the *Virgin in Glory* by Karl Bryullov and Fyodor Bruni, and the iconostasis with its columns in malachite and lapis-lazuli,

mosaics, and the gilded sculpture of *Christ in Glory* by Pyotr Klodt.

Numbers . . .

Saint Isaac's Cathedral stuns with its size. It is 111.5 meters in length and 97.6 in width; it can hold 14,000 people and weighs about 300,000 tons; it is decorated with 112 granite columns, the lower 48 of which are 17 meters in height and weigh 130 tons each. The walls are 5 meters thick in some places. A staircase of 562 steps leads to the dome: its gilded cross soars to 101.88 meters, 30 meters higher than the caravel at the top of the Admiralty spire. About 100 kg of gold were required for gilding the enormous dome. The works of art in the cathedral (sculptures, paintings, and mosaics) are 382 in number. Each wing of the enormous, artistic bronze portals weighs about 10 tons. The bronze reliefs on the pediments measure 40 x 6.50 meters. The marvelous mosaics in the interior are made of enameled tiles in 28,000 different tones of color and cover a surface area of 600 square meters. Forty-three different types of minerals were used in the building of the cathedral: granite for the plinth, Russian, Italian, and French marbles for the floors, malachite and lapis-lazuli for the columns of the iconostasis.

SAINT ISAAC'S SQUARE

With Saint Isaac's Cathedral on its north side and its southern end dominated by the Mariinskiy Palace across the great Blue Bridge over the Moyka, this great square centering on the monument to Nicholas I is home to a number of palaces more than worthy of mention; for example, the **Grand Hotel Astoria-Angleterre** and the **former German Embassy**, both built in 1911, one across from the other.

Equestrian Statue of Nicholas I
The equestrian statue of Czar Nicholas I, to a model by the sculptor Pyotr Klodt, was erected in 1859 at the center of the square.
It is an equestrian monument unique in its genre (6 meters in height!) since it poses on only two points of support: the horse's hind legs. The czar is shown in the uniform of the Horse Guards, wearing a helmet with an eagle; the rider's pose is haughty. It was clearly the sculptor's intent to point up Nicholas' passion for the military style. The pedestal is decorated with **allegorical statues**: **Faith** (holding the Cross and the Gospels), **Wisdom** (with a mirror), **Justice** (with the scales), and **Might** (with sword and lance). The lineaments of the faces of these figures are those of Nicholas I's wife and daughters.
On the base, impressive **high reliefs** relate episodes from the reign of the czar. For example, Nicholas' speech to the court dignitaries after suppression of the

Decembrist insurrection of 14 December 1825; the charge against the angry crowd in Sennaya Square in 1831 during the so-called "Cholera" or Russia-Poland Revolt; the ceremony conferring on the official M. Speranskiy the Order of Saint Andrew in 1832, on occasion of publication of the ponderosa "complete collection of Russian imperial law," and the czar's 1851 visit to the bridge for the new railway linking Saint Petersburg with Moscow.

On these pages, the equestrian statue of Czar Nicholas II, in Saint Isaac's Square, and two details of the base.

Circus!

The Russian school of circus is famous throughout the world, but maybe not everyone knows that the first permanent construction for hosting a circus was built in Saint Petersburg, on the Fontanka not far from the Engineers' Castle. Circuses had appeared in Russia in the early 1800's, but the building destined to house the circus of the Italian Giuseppe Ciniselli was not raised until 1876-1877. Yet today, this historical building is the home of the Saint Petersburg theater. It is not only a performance venue, however: it is also a school where animal training is taught and practiced.

Lobanov-Rostovskiy Palace

The building across from the corner of the east facade of Saint Isaac's Cathedral, built on a triangular plan in 1817-1820 to designs by Auguste Montferrand for Count A. Lobanov-Rostovskiy, is worthy of note.

The main facade, facing the Admiralty, is embellished with a solemn portico of eight Corinthian columns.

To the sides of the center arch are **white marble lions** on granite pedestals. These are the very works by the sculptor Paolo Triscorni extolled by Pushkin in his poem "The Bronze Horseman."

Mariinskiy Palace

The southern portion of Saint Isaac's Square, across the Blue Bridge, is occupied by the building

The Lobanov-Rostovskiy Palace and the Mariinskiy Palace, today the home of the Saint Petersburg City Hall.

that housed the former Ratusha (Town Hall); it was later the head-quarters of the Soviet (Congress) of People's Deputies and is now the home of the Saint Petersburg City Hall.

Until 1830, this was the site of the two-story home built by the architect J. Vallin de la Mothe in the 1760's for major-general Count Chernischev, a dignitary at Catherine's court. In the late 18th century, by order of Paul I, who had just ascended the throne, the building was marked with the Bourbon lily (emblem of the deposed French dynasty) and was given to the Prince of Condé who had sought refuge in Russia at the time of the French Revolution.

About halfway through the 1820's, the Ministry of War obtained the building for use as the headquarters of the Guards' Non-Commissioned Officers Academy. In 1834, the distinguished Russian poet Mikhail Lermontov graduated from this school.

The school was moved to the outskirts of the city in 1839.

Czar Nicholas I intended making a precious gift to his daughter, Maria; thus in 1839-1844 the court architect A. Stakenschneider was set to work building Mariinskiy Palace (that is, "of Maria") on the site that formerly hosted the academy.

The State Council was moved to the Mariinskiy Palace after the heirs of Grand Duchess Maria granted the palace to the state in 1884.

A few steps away was the Winter Garden, replaced, in 1906-1907, by the meeting premises for the State Council, which was formally the country's highest legislative organ.

After the revolution of February 1917, Mariinskiy Palace was for a short period the seat of the provisional government until it was moved, in the summer of the same year, to the Winter Palace.

From the vestibule of the main entrance, a white marble staircase decorated with **stuccowork** and **statues** of ancient warriors leads to the first floor and the grand **Festival Hall**. The hall is decorated with pillars of dark red Italian marble and a sculptural **frieze** showing episodes from Homer's *Iliad*. Next to the Festival Hall—the most striking room in the palace, thanks to its decor—is a rotunda of white marble decorated with Corinthian columns that form two loggias.

The Grand Hotel Astoria-Angleterre, in saint Isaac's Square and the Blue Bridge with one of the nearby Neo-Renaissance buildings.

The Blue Bridge

About a hundred meters wide (but much shorter), the Blue Bridge over the Moyka is actually the continuation to the south of Saint Isaac's Square. Until 1861 it was the site of the serfs' market. Near the bridge are two lovely **Neo-Renaissance** style buildings, raised in 1844 to plans by Nikolai Efimov.

THE NEVSKIY PROSPEKT
between Moyka and Fontanka

*T*he look of this famous boulevard is polyhedral, with 18th-century buildings alternating with other built only in the 20th. Until the 19th century the Fontanka river was the southern limit of the city, and for this reason the buildings on the Nevskiy Prospekt between the Admiralty and the Fontanka were part of the city long before those found between the Anichkov Bridge and the Alexander Nevsky Monastery. These relatively more recent constructions are much more varied in appearance than those within the old borders. The width of the major artery goes from 25 meters (between the Admiralty and the Moyka river) to sixty (near the Gostinyy Dvor bazaar. The Prospekt was renovated after the war: the streetcar lines were removed, the underpasses and the subway stations were built, and green tree landscaping appeared in front of Gostinyy Dvor and in the adjacent streets.

A view of the Nevskiy Prospekt.

History

The Nevskiy Prospekt stretches for 4260 meters between the Admiralty and the Alexander Nevsky Monastery. It is the city's main street—and its busiest.

Its history goes back to the very first years of Saint Petersburg. The villages along the banks of the Neva were linked to the other Russian centers mainly by the Novgorod road, which ran along the route of today's Ligovskiy Boulevard.

When the Admiralty shipyard entered into operation, wagons loaded with iron, canvas, rope, oak planks—in short, with everything the shipyard needed—began to rumble into the city along the Novgorod road, and were able to reach the Admiralty only by making long detours along narrow lanes that had certainly not been designed to handle such traffic. For this reason it was decided to open a street from the Admiralty to the Novgorod road: the "Great Perspective Road."

In 1738 it was decided to give the name of Nevskiy Prospekt to the stretch between the Admiralty and the Alexander Nevsky Monastery.

By the second half of the 18th century this was the city's main thoroughfare. Along it were built a myriad of churches, palaces and mansions, markets, and public buildings. Construction of apartment houses, hotels, and banks began in the first years of the 20th century. Construction of the Moscow Station (formerly known as Nikolaevskiy Station), in the mid-1800's, only added to the animation of the Nevskiy Prospekt.

The facade of the Baroque Stroganov Palace, a masterpiece by Francesco Bartolomeo Rastrelli.

At No. 20 on the even-numbered side of the Nevskiy Prospekt is the **Dutch Church** with its elegant Neo-Classical portico. The church, built in 1834-1839 by the architect P. Jacquot, features a high relief of two **angels with the Gospels** in the tympanum of the pediment.

Stroganov Palace

On the other side of the Nevskiy Prospekt, at No. 17, is the palace that belonged to Count Sergei Stroganov, one of the richest men in the city of his time. This elaborate work by the architect Francesco Bartolomeo Rastrelli was built in 1752-1754. The building is decorated with columns and sculptures; the stuccowork ornaments are mostly located in the central portion. The arch of the entrance portal (ornamented with sculpted **lion masks**) supports a four-column portico that in turn supports the bizarre pediment, typical of the Baroque, with the **Stroganov family coat-of-arms**: two sables raised on their hind legs holding in their front paws a shield cut in half by a bandoleer with three lance blades. The sables represent Siberia, in the union of which region with Russia the ancestors of the Stroganovs participated. The frame of the first-floor window, above the arch, is high-

lighted by **atlantes** in relief. The other first-floor windows are decorated with **lion masks and medallions with a man's profile** in relief. The ceremonial halls were located on the first floor of the palace.

The Stroganov Palace is now a museum structure, a section of the Russian Museum, used for **temporary exhibits**.

Almost facing the palace are Nos. 22 and 24 of the Prospekt. Between them, and set a little back, is **Saint Peter's Lutheran Church**, the facade of which overlooks the Prospekt. The central portion of the facade is cut by the impressive arch of the portal surmounted by an open loggia. In the same place, at the first-floor level, are sculpted the figures of the **Evangelists** in bas-relief. Two soaring towers mark the corners of the main facade and the sides of the center sculpture (**an angel with the Cross**). The church was built in 1833-1838 by the architect A. Bryullov.

The palaces at Nos. 22 and 24, mentioned above, are from the same time. In the 1830's, No. 22 hosted the well-known bookstore of A. Smirdin, who was the first to publish the books of Pushkin and Krylov.

The majestic Cathedral of Our Lady of Kazan.

THE CATHEDRAL OF OUR LADY OF KAZAN

The Cathedral of Our Lady of Kazan, the most beautiful edifice on the Nevskiy Prospekt, was built in the years 1801-1811 to plans by Andrei Voronikhin. The art of this great architect, from a family of serfs, opened the age of the flowering of Russian architecture in the first half of the 19th century.

The Square and the Colonnade
Voronikhin created a majestic building, clearly inspired by Saint Peter's Basilica in Rome: it is 71.6 meters in height and as much as 72.5 meters in length; its long axis and most important facade run parallel to the Nevskiy Prospekt. The cathedral, with its semicircular colonnade (96 Corinthian columns, 13 meters in height each), delimits one of the most solemn of the city's squares. The gently-curving colonnade seems, according to your point of view, to be now an airy transparent fence, now a solid wall of columns in yellow calcareous stone. At the ends of the colonnade on the Nevskiy Prospekt are gigantic bas-reliefs (about 15 meters in length and almost 2 meters

The Miraculous Icon

The icon of the Madonna of Kazan is one of the most widely-venerated in Russia. It was found in 1579 in Kazan immediately after the city had been retaken from the Tartars by Ivan the Terrible; this victory liberated Russia from Mongol oppression. Tradition has it that in 1612 the icon aided in driving the Polish out of Moscow and in 1812 the defeat of Napoleon's army. The original icon disappeared in 1904 from the Saint Petersburg cathedral and has not been heard of since.

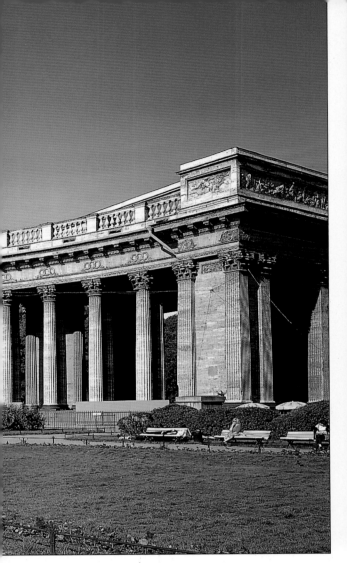

The monument to Mikhail Kutuzov, in front of one of the wings of the colonnade.

high) inspired by the Bible. The left relief, the work of the well-known Russian sculptor I. Martos, shows **Moses Parting the Waters**; the right relief, by I. Prokofiev, is of the **Bronze Serpent**.

The niches of the north portico (facing the Nevskiy Prospekt) shelter bronze statues of the **prince and saint Vladimir** (during whose reign in Kiev, in 988, Russia was named) by S. Pimenov, **Saint John the Baptist** by I. Martos, **Saint Alexander Nevsky** by S. Pimenov, and **Saint Andrew** by V. Demut-Malinovskiy.

The Interior

The decoration of the interior of the cathedral is also of high artistic value. Of particular note, the **56 monolithic columns** in red granite and the **mosaic pavement** made with marble from the Carelia region. Collaborating on the decorations were V. Borovikovskiy, O. Kiprenskiy, and other great early 19th-century Russian masters.

After the victory over Napoleon's troops in the War of 1812, the Cathedral of Our Lady of Kazan became a sort of monument to Russian military glory. And thus, it is here that we also find, on the exact spot where he prayed before leaving for the front, the sepulchre of Field Marshall Mikhail Kutuzov who died in 1813.

In 1837, the year of the 25th anniversary of Napoleon's expulsion from Russia, the **monuments to M. Kutuzov and M. Barclay de Tolly**, two leaders of the Russian troops, were erected in front of the cathedral. The statues were sculpted by B. Orlovskiy; the red granite pedestals were produced to plans by V. Stasov. In the Soviet period, the church was the seat of a museum of atheism; in 1999 it was returned to its original function.

A semicircular plaza opens in front of the cathedral; it is surrounded by a splendid **iron fence** 171 meters in length created to plans by Voronikhin in 1811-1812.

The House of Books
(The Singer Building)

The unique Singer Building (1902-1904) was designed in early Modernist style by the architect P. Syuzor for the branch office of the famous American sewing machine company. The building features facades with large windows framed in shining granite and decorated with the *bronze statues* by the Estonian artist A. Adamson symbolizing Industry. Today, the building hosts Saint Petersburg's largest bookstore and a number of publishing houses. The glass globe on the conical corner tower is supported by the *Allegories of Navigation*.

At No. 30, on the other side of the Griboedov Canal, we find a building constructed in the late 18th century hosting the *Small Hall of the Philharmonia*, a center for chamber music that is still very popular in the city; in the early 19th century it was the most important auditorium in Saint Petersburg, where the greatest Russian musicians and the great western European composers (H. Berlioz, R. Wagner, F. Liszt, and J. Strauss) performed and were represented.

The Singer Building and a detail of the facade.

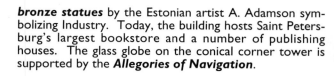

The Firefighters' Tower and the Former Duma

A many-storied pentagonal tower, with a clock, rises at the corner between the Prospekt and Dumskaya Street. The former Duma Tower was built in 1799-1804 as a watchtower for fires; for a certain time it received and transmitted the "optical telegraph" signals.

The Duma (center of local government) had its seat in the buildings topped by a tower on the Dumskaya Street side. The building was raised in the late 18th century but later underwent so many modifications that the original look has been lost.

Catholic Church of Saint Catherine

The Roman Catholic Church of Saint Catherine (1763-1783, architects J. Vallin de la Mothe e A. Rinaldi) is the final resting place of the last king of Poland, Stanislaw-August Poniatowsky. He abdicated in 1795 and lived in Saint Petersburg until the end of his days. Also buried here is the French general Jean Moreau. When Napoleon was proclaimed emperor, Moreau emigrated from France and after Napoleon's troops had invaded Russia (1812) he came to Saint Petersburg, where he was awarded permission to fight against the French. The church is a splendid example of architectural style spanning the Baroque and the Classical.

Further along, on the same side and half-hidden among other buildings, is the **Armenian Church**, a work in Russian Classical style (1771-1780) by Yuriy Velten.

Gostinyy Dvor

On the odd-numbered side of the Prospekt stands a very special building that occupies an entire block. The construction, with its continuous lines of arcades on two floors, is the Gostinyy Dvor (House of Merchants). Built in 1757-1785 by F. B. Rastrelli and J. Vallin de la Mothe, it is the largest gallery of outlets in all of Saint Petersburg. Its facades face on four streets and its perimeter exceeds one kilometer. The Gostinyy Dvor, ancient on the outside and modern within, is very popular and always crowded.

The Passage Arcade at No. 48, with its three floors of shops, is another great shopping mall. Among the "historical" shops are Sever, located at No. 44 in a building dating to 1909-1910, and, at No. 56, the opulent Eliseevskiy, built in 1903-1910 and featuring the original early 20th-century furnishings.

Ostrovskiy Square and "Architect Rossi Street"

Past Sadovaya Street we come to Ostrovskiy Square. The beautiful **monument to Catherine II**, the majestic National Library building, the light, slim pavilions of the garden of the Anichkov Palace, and the solemn edifice of the Aleksandrinskiy Theater make up one of Saint Petersburg's most beautiful architectural complexes. Teatralnaya Street, behind the theater, is unique in its genre: one of the city's most "theatrical," in the Soviet period it was given the name of its designer Carlo Rossi

The former Duma building with the Firefighters' Tower and the Church of Saint Catherine.

(Ulitsa Zodchevo Rossi). It was opened in 1828-1834; it is lined by two identical buildings painted yellow and decorated with white columns like the theater. The street is as wide as the buildings are high: 22 meters, making the transversal section a perfect square. The length of the buildings is ten times their height: 220 meters. The street leads into the beautiful Lomonosov Square, designed by Rossi, on the Fontanka.

Aleksandrinskiy Theater

Construction of the Aleksandrinskiy Theater (Pushkin Theater during the Soviet parenthesis) began in 1828 to plans by Carlo Rossi. The main facade, completed in 1832, is decorated with a six-columned loggia raised on a high rustic-order ground floor. A frieze of garlands and theatrical masks runs all around the building. Two small niches at the sides of the loggia host the *statues of the Muses Melpomene and Terpsichore*. The attic floor is surmounted by the *chariot of Apollo*, who holds in one hand the crown awarded to the winners of the contests and in the other the lyre, from whose strings the god extracted divine music. Ever since its founding, the Aleksandrinskiy Theater (from the name of Nicholas I's wife) has played an important role in the social life of the country as the standard-bearer of Russian dramaturgy.

Russian National Library

In 1796-1801, the architect E. Sokolov built the first library building at the corner with Sadovaya Street. In 1828-1834, Rossi added a new building, the main facade of which faces Ostrovskiy Square. The walls of the new addition were decorated with *bas-reliefs* and *sculptures* of scientists, orators, philosophers, and writers of antiquity, dominated by the figure of Minerva. In the late 19th century, Rossi's edifice was augmented by addition of a building, designed by E. Vorotilov, at the corner of the street named for Ivan Krylov, the narrator of fables who for many years worked in the library. Saint Petersburg's library is one of the world's largest (with 25 million volumes) and the second-largest in Russia. The Russian holding is the world's most complete collection of editions of books printed in Russia.

The Aleksandrinskiy Theater, designed by Carlo Rossi, and artists at work making portraits of the tourists in search of a personalized souvenir, in the Ostrovskiy Square park.

Anichkov Palace

Anichkov Palace (called thus from the nearby bridge) was built by the architects M. Zemtsov, F. B. Rastrelli, and G. Dmitriev in 1741-1754 for the czarina Elizabeth, who intended to give it to Count Razumovskiy to whom she was secretly married. In the 1770's it was partially rebuilt by the architect I. Starov. The main facade faces the Fontanka. In 1817-1818, Carlo Rossi renovated the palace rooms and restructured the adjacent areas, considerably reducing the area dedicated to the gardens we see from Ostrovskiy Square. The fencing around the gardens and the two *pavilions* were also built in accordance with Rossi's plans.

Belosel'skiy-Belozerskiy Palace

Across the bridge, at the corner with the Fontanka river embankment, is the interesting home of Prince Belosel'skiy-Belozerskiy, built in 1847-1848 by the architect A. Stakenschneider. It was later owned by many relatives of the czar. The forms of the Baroque style predominate in the eclectic architecture of this palace.

The elegant Eliseevskiy shop, the Anichkov Bridge with one of Klodt's four famous horses, a detail of the Armenian Church, and the Belosel'skiy-Belozerskiy Palace.

*T*he short Mikhailovskaya Street opens to the left of the Nevskiy Prospekt, connecting it with the **Arts Square complex**, one of Saint Petersburg's finest, the work of Carlo Rossi. The buildings around the square host three museums and three theaters, including the celebrated **Russian Museum**, the **M. Mussorgsky Maly** ("small") **Opera and Ballet The-**ater, and the **Great Hall of the D. Shostakovich Philharmonia**. The complex occupies a vast area between the Griboedov Canal and the Moyka river. In the late 18th and early 19th centuries the area that is now the Arts Square park was isolated and wooded. And in the first years of the 1800's a castle was built there for Grand Duke Mikhail, the fourth son of Paul I.

In Russian Classicist style, the Mikhailovskiy Palace, home of the prestigious Russian Museum, with its front garden.

On the next page, the monument to Alexander Pushkin, by M. Anikushin at the center of the small garden on Arts Square, showing the poet reciting his verses, and two details of the Russian Museum building.

MIKHAILOVSKIY PALACE AND THE RUSSIAN MUSEUM

The Mikhailovskiy Palace was built by the architect Rossi in 1819-1825. The two wings for the service facilities at the sides of the palace delimit the gardens, wich are ringed by a cast-iron railing, one of the city's most beautiful. The pillars of the gates are decorated with military breastplates. On wide, gently sloping ramps, carriages came up to right under the portico which is surmounted, on the floor above, by eight columns with Corinthian capitals. At the center of the portico is a wide granite staircase flanked by two statues of **lions**.

Sculpture was lavishly used in the decoration of the facade of the Mikhailovskiy Palace and its interiors. The ornamentation of the vestibule, the **grand staircase**, and the **White Hall**, come down to us in their original aspect, are among the most beautiful examples of Russian Classicism anywhere.

In the 1890's, the palace was rearranged to host the Russian Museum, opened to visitors in 1898. The exhibit rooms are in the Mikhailovskiy Palace and the two adjacent buildings in the direction of the Griboedov Canal: the **Rossi Wing** and the **Benois Wing** at the corner with

A Neo-Classical Square

Carlo Rossi designed the facades of all the buildings encircling Arts Square. Each owner was allowed to build on his land as he saw fit, but there was one very severe rule: the facades of the buildings had to respect Rossi's Neo-Classical designs. In the late 19th century, however, the rule was no longer always strictly respected; one side of Mikhailovskaya Street was rebuilt and today the Grand Hotel Europe building contrasts with the rest of the complex.

the canal. To these buildings have been added the Marble Palace, the Engineers' Castle, and the Stroganov Palace.

The almost five thousand items on exhibit at the museum (only a small portion of the museum's holdings, which count more than 300 thousand works of art), are arranged according to chronological-monographic criteria to unreel to visitors the history and the treasures of Russian art from the 11th century to our times.

The ancient Russian art section presents works by the famous Andrei Rubliov, by Dionisiy, and by Simon Usciakov.

Eighteenth-century art is represented by the canvases of I. Nikitin, F. Rokotov, D. Levitskiy, V. Borovikovskiy, and other great masters. And again, works by F. Sciubin, M. Kozlovskiy, I. Martos, and other eminent sculptors.

Of especial historical and artistic value is **Rubliov's icon of the Apostle Paul**, representing the saint holding a book, always his attribute. Rubliov's image of the learned theologian is that of a wise man who while old is nevertheless full of spiritual vigor. The eminent early-18th century master of Russian painting

Ivan Nikitin created the best **portrait of Peter I** painted from life; the **bronze bust of Peter I**, a work by Bartolomeo Carlo Rastrelli, the father of the great architect and an eminent sculptor in his own right, exactly translates the image of the czar; but differently from Nikitin's painting, Rastrelli's Peter is quite strongly idealized and pompous. Also by Rastrelli, the splendid sculptural composition of the czarina **Anna Ivanovna with an Arab Boy**.

Sciubin's works, like the **bust of the czar Paul I**, must be considered masterpieces of sculptural portraiture.

Splendid the elegant, intimate portraits by Rokotov, a former serf who rose to become an academician of painting. Also outstanding is the collection of canvases by early 19th-century painters, including the Romantic portraits by O. Kiprenskiy and the landscapes by S. Scedrin and I. Aiazovsky.

I. Aiazovsky:
The Tenth Wave *(1850).*

K. Bryullov:
The Last Day of
Pompeii *(1833).*

A. Ivanov:
The Appearance of
Christ before the People
(1830's).

On the facing page, the czarina Anna Ivanovna with an Arab Boy, *a sculpture in bronze by Bartolomeo Carlo Rastrelli, and the splendid White Hall designed by Carlo Rossi.*

Karl Bryullov's painting **The Last Day of Pompeii**, which caused true furor in the West, brought the painter great renown. Together with the works of the landscape artists already mentioned, and A. Ivanov's penetrating **The Appearance of Christ before the People**, the paintings and portraits by these masters marked the great awakening of 19th-century Russian artistic culture.

The visitor's attention will also be drawn to the works of A. Venezianov and V. Tropinin and the acute satiric canvases of P. Fedotov (the spirit of whose art was further developed by V. Perov).

The works of the many other painters and sculptors who contributed to glorifying Russian art in these decades also grace the halls of the museum

The splendid portraits by V. Serov and the works of N. Rerikh, and B. Kustodiev brought new glory to Russian culture in the late 19th and early 20th centuries. In the Soviet art section the visitor will come to know the works of A. Rylov, K. Petrov-Vodkin, A. Deineka, and A. Samokhvalov. Of especial interest are the canvases by the avant-garde painters **V. Kandinsky**, **P. Filonov**, and **K. Malevich**; these are unique items but at the same

V. M. Vasnetsov:
A Knight at the Crossroads
(1882).

A. N. Samokhvalov:
The Girl in Football-Jersey
(1932).

time typical of the modern art of the time, when innovative research and creative experimentation were bywords.

The exhibit halls and deposits of the museum are also the repositories of precious collections of **decorative and applied art**.

Russian Ethnographic Museum

The collections of this museum, which is rightly considered the greatest in all Russia, count more than 250 thousand items relating to the life and art of more **than 130 peoples and ethnic groups** of the former Soviet Union. The exhibit rooms present traditional costumes, religious articles and items from daily life, and decorative and artistic works. The museum building stands alongside that of the Russian Museum, on the corner of Sadovaya Street.

B. Kustodiev:
The Merchant's Wife *(1915).*

A. Benois:
Parade under Paul I *(1907).*

K. Malevich: To Harvest *(1928-1929).*

P. Filonov: Animals *(1930).*

V. Kandinsky: Blue Ridge *(1917).*

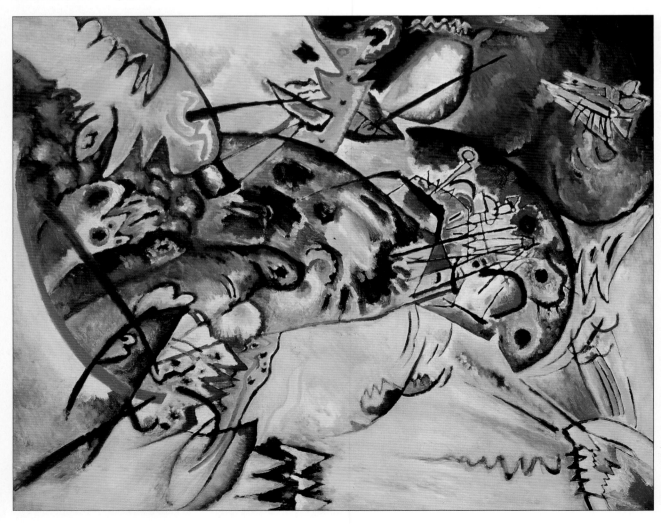

K. Malevich: Apple Trees in Blossom *(1904).*

Music and Saint Petersburg

Music has always played an important role in the life and culture of the city, which was the birthplace or residence of many great composers: *Mikhail Glinka, Anton Rubinstein, Nikolai Rimsky-Korsakov, Modest Mussorgsky, Alexander Borodin, Pyotr Ilyich Tchiaikovsky, Igor Stravinsky,* and *Dmitri Shostakovich.*

The **Mussorgsky Theater of Opera and Ballet**, on the west side of Arts Square, was built in 1831-1833 by the architect A. Bryullov in style with the beautiful plan for the square and Mikhailovskaya Street drawn up by Carlo Rossi.

On the opposite side of the square, in the corner building that also faces on Brodsky Street, is the **Great Hall of the Dmitri Shostakovich Philharmonia**. The building was raised in 1834-1839 by the architect P. Jacquot (with Rossi's facades!) for the Assembly of Nobles. It saw a number of famous premieres, including Beethoven's *Missa Solemnis (Solemn Mass)* and Tchaikovsky's *Pathetique*, directed by the author. In 1921, the Petrograd State Philharmonia was opened. From here, in 1942, when the city had been under siege for 11 months by the Germans, the radio transmitted Shostakovich's *Seventh Symphony "Leningrad"* to the entire nation.

The M. Mussorgsky Opera and Ballet Theater.

RESURRECTION CHURCH OF OUR SAVIOR (CHURCH ON SPILLED BLOOD)

The Resurrection Church of Our Savior was built in 1883-1907 on the embankment of the Ekaterininskiy Canal (now the Griboedov Canal), on the spot where on 1 March 1881 the conspirator I. Grinevit-skiy mortally wounded Czar Alexander II (hence the other name, by which the church is better known: the Church on Spilled Blood). The building, by the architect A. Parland, is in the arabesqued Russian Revival style and in many ways copies the forms and the compositive methods of the famous Cathedral of the Intercession on Red Square in Moscow, better known as the Saint Basil's, an unsurpassed architectural monument of ancient Russia. The outer walls of the church are clad with profiled glazed bricks, ceramic tiles, and maiolicas; the domes are multicolored; the entrance portals on the north and south sides were built with balcony vestibules on granite columns.

Details of the exterior of the Resurrection Church of Our Savior (Church on Spilled Blood), showing the chromatic and decorative variety of various elements.
On the facing page, a view of the church on the banks of the Griboedov Canal.

The pediments of the four entrance balconies are decorated with **mosaic panels** representing evangelical subjects, made to sketches by V. Vasnetsov. The sketch for the panel underneath the roofing arch of the north facade is the work of M. Nesterov. The church has a single nave with three apses; **polychrome marbles** from Italy and **natural Russian stones** were used for the decorations of the interior. The **mosaics** are the principal decorative elements of the both the interior and the exterior of the church, whose building created dissonance with the surrounding Russian Classical architecture—but for exactly this reason it lends an important accent to the style of the city.

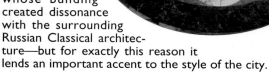

Images of the interior of the Resurrection Church of Our Savior (Church on Spilled Blood) with the iconostasis (above) and the baldachin erected on the site the czar was assassinated (left). The walls and ceilings of the church are a veritable cloak of mosaics: top left, Saint Alexander Nevsky; right, Saints Clement and Carpus.

Crafts

A dip into the most typical Russian handcrafts? Here we go: the appealing *matryoshka* nested dolls, known and loved worldwide, bowls, spoons, boxes, trays, and variously-colored and gilded wooden eggs; warm fur busbies; elegant chess-sets for interminable games, and jewelry for all tastes, studded with the semiprecious stones of the Urals.

Choosing a single souvenir to take home is no easy matter.

MIKHAILOVSKIY
(OR THE ENGINEERS') CASTLE

Beyond the southern fence of the Summer Garden is the Mikhailovskiy or Engineers' Castle, one of Saint Petersburg's most beautiful buildings.

After the death of Catherine II in 1796, her son Paul I was afraid to live in the Winter Palace, seeing as he did plots against his life at every turn. He thus ordered construction of a new palace that could better defend him from his enemies. It was named in honor of the Archangel Michael, who as patron of the celestial hosts aroused the sympathies of the diffident Czar Paul I.

The castle was built in 1797-1800 to plans by the great architect Vasiliy Bazhenov, who died in 1799: work continued under V. Brenna, who made his own changes to the plans. The secret passages inside the palace, the bastions, and the moats with drawbridges seemed to Paul to provide sufficient protection against backstairs plots. But he lived for only 40 days in his new residence. He died on the night of 11 March 1801, suffocated by his courtiers.

Each of the four facades of the castle is architecturally different from the others. The most flamboyant is the south facade, with in the central portion a portico with four red marble columns crowned by a pediment which is in turn surmounted by the attic. The Paros marble sculpture in the tympanum of the pediment is by the brothers Pietro and Gioacchino Staggi. Two **obelisks** in grey Siberian marble, with military mono-

grams and armor, underline the solemn aspect of the main palace entrance.

The west facade (on the Sadovaya Street side) is emphasized by the **court church**, dedicated to Archangel Michael, with its portal decorated with four Ionic half-columns and two granite staircases at the entrance. Other Ionic columns support the balcony on the first floor, where Paul's library was located.

The aspect of the north facade is more reserved: here, the center portion is framed by two jutting portions underneath a high attic adorned with sculptures. Between the projections is a row of paired Doric columns in pink Olonets marble. The wide staircase is decorated with **sculptures of Hercules**.

The east facade is enlivened by a curving projection formed by the walls of the oval dining room.

During the far-reaching restoration work carried on in this district of the city in 1820 under the direction of Carlo Rossi, the canals that surrounded the castle were filled and the drawbridges demolished. In 1823 the Central Engineering School was moved here and the building was called the "Engineers' Castle." The list of illustrious students at this school includes the writer F. Dostoevsky, the well-known Russian composer C. Cui, and the scientist and technician P. Jablochkov (inventor of the lamp that was the basis for the first electrical lighting system put into practical use).

In 1800, a **monument to Peter I** by the sculptor B. C. Rastrelli (father of the famous architect) was installed in front of the main entrance to the castle. It was the

first equestrian statue ever made in Russia. Peter is portrayed as a triumphal emperor, powerful and terrible. The base, faced with marble slabs in shades of pink, green, and white, is ornamented with bronze bas-reliefs illustrating the key victories in the Great Northern War conducted by Peter I: the **victory at Poltava** (1709) and the **victorious naval battle of Cape Hangut** (today, Kanka), in 1714. By order of Paul I, the base was engraved with the words "To his great-grandfather from his great-grandson" and the date of the unveiling of the monument, "1800." Today, the historical rooms, including the room in which the czar was assassinated, are part of the historical museum itinerary; other rooms, belonging to the Russian Museum, are used for **temporary exhibits**.

On the facing page, the north facade of the Engineers' Castle, overlooking the Summer Garden.
On this page, a detail of the north facade of the Castle with the sculptures that adorn the attic, and details of signs, bridges, and streetlamps near the building.

IN AND NEAR THE FIELD OF MARS

The opening pages of the history of Saint Petersburg are inextricably linked to the Peter and Paul Fortress, since the city was edified on the right bank of the Neva, under wartime fire, in the shadow of the fortified walls. As the Russian troops met with more and more success, the left bank, called the "Moscow area," was also built up. This complex, which began to take form after 1710, is one of the city's largest and includes the green **Summer and Mikhailovskiy Gardens**, the solemn **Field of Mars Square**, and a series of splendid **monuments** to form a great single historical and artistic unit.

The courtyard of the Marble Palace with the monument to Czar Alexander III by Paolo Trubetskoy.

The Marble Palace seen from the Neva.

THE MARBLE PALACE

The Marble Palace was built (1768-1785) to plans by Rinaldi in the northwestern corner of the Field of Mars for Grigoriy Orlov, head of the conspiracy that brought Catherine II to the throne.

It is a building of considerable architectural value, since it marks the transition between the Baroque and Russian Classicism. The facades, on the Neva Embankment, the Marble Alley, and the Field of Mars, are drawn with clean, essential lines. The walls are clad in grey granite; the first and second floors feature Corinthian pillars in light pink marble. On the facade looking out on the courtyard is a window larger than the entrance arch; the gentle lines of its decoration are closer to the Baroque than to the Classical.

Thirty-two different qualities of marble were used for the walls and decoration of the interiors. The top Russian sculptors of the late 18th century, F. Sciubin and M. Kozlovskiy, created the sculptural decorations of the palace. To the east, the courtyard is closed off by the service building built in the 1840's to plans by A. Bryullov. Interesting the **bas-relief frieze** (49 meters long and 1.7 high), made by Pyotr Klodt, on the west facade of this building: the scenes all revolve around the theme of the horse serving man. In 1937 the Marble Palace became the local seat of the Central Lenin Museum. Many rooms were adapted to house the exhibits, but the most beautiful interiors from the artistic point of view were preserved intact. Today, the palace is home to a section of the Russian Museum, with works by foreign artists who stayed in Russia and works by such modern artists as **Picasso**, **Andy Warhol**, **Roy Lichtenstein**, **Jean-Michel Basquiat**, and **Ilya Kabakov**.

On these pages, the Summer Palace with the Fontanka river, the lovely grille along the Neva, and Peter I's study on the ground floor of the building.

THE SUMMER PALACE

This two-story building, built in 1710-1714 to Domenico Trezzini's designs, was the city's first palace. The layout is identical on all the floors: six halls, a kitchen, a corridor, and a room for the officials on duty or for the ladies of the court. The ground-floor rooms were Peter the Great's; those on the first floor belonged to his wife Catherine. The *majolica-tiled kitchen*, the atrium, decorated with artistic *engravings*, the furnishings of the *Green Study* on the ground floor, the majolica stoves, and the *painted ceilings* have all come down to us in excellent condition. Among the exhibit pieces in the palace-museum are items from Peter I's original wardrobe and the lathes built by A. Nartov, an illustrious mechanical genius who worked in Peter's time.

In 1839, the south entrance to the garden was enhanced with a *decorative vase* in pink porphyry, 4.85 meters tall, sculpted in the Swedish city of Elfdalen. The vase, composed of five parts made separately, was a gift from the king of Sweden Karl Friederich Johann to Czar Nicholas I. In 1855, a *monument to Ivan Krylov*, Russia's most famous narrator of fables, was unveiled in the garden. Interesting the pedestal on which Pyotr Klodt, author of the monument, portrayed the characters in Krylov's fables in high relief.

Here and on the facing page, images of the Summer Garden with several of the many statues that adorn it; in the large photograph, the sculptural group entitled Peace and Abundance.

THE SUMMER GARDEN

On an area of almost 12 hectares, the garden is separated from the Neva Embankment by a splendid *railing* dating to 1770-1784, designed by Yuriy Velten (son of Peter I's cook) and P. Egorov. Thirty-six *monolithic columns* decorated with vases and urns support a finely elegant iron grille. The garden was created in 1704 in the style called "uniform": its layout features precise geometrical lines, the paths were framed with well-pruned trees. The garden was adorned with scores of fountains inspired by Aesop's fables, which were not rebuilt after they were destroyed by the 1777 flood. Rare plants and flowers and marble sculptures were imported from all over Russia and western Europe to decorate the garden. Peter the Great, who dreamed of creating a garden "more beautiful than that of the King of France in Versailles," had no qualms about expenses and even purchased an ancient statue of Venus found in Italy: the Summer Garden, which owes its name to the palace of the same name, became the center of social and political life in the Saint Petersburg of the times.

The Summer Garden is fascinating not only for its shady allées (with more than 10,000 trees) but also for its many *statues*. In front of the facade of the Summer Palace is the allegorical sculptural group entitled *Peace and Abundance*, sculpted in 1722 by P. Baratta on commission from Peter I: it is an allegory of the Russian victory over Sweden in the Great Northern War. Abundance (Russia) is a young woman holding in her left hand a cornucopia and in her right an upended torch, symbol of the ended war. Alongside there stands Winged Victo-

ry, with one hand crowning Russia in victorious laurels and with the other holding a palm frond, symbol of peace. Her foot rests on a slaughtered lion (symbol of Sweden). Another beautiful sculpture is the group entitled *Eros and Psyche*, located near the Swan Canal that links the Neva and Moyka rivers. A 17th-century work by an unknown author, it is a typical example of the Baroque style. One of the first sculptures installed in the garden is the bust of *Christine Queen of Sweden* (1626-1689): a no longer young woman, with a capricious set to her lips and deep wrinkles on her face; her precious collier is partly hidden by lace. Another ancient work is the *bust of Jan Sobieski* (1624-1696), the king of Sweden whose fame derives from his victories over the Turks. The sculptor, while faithfully reproducing the king's features, lent to the image that touch of supreme beauty typical of official portraiture of the late 17th century. Another attention-catcher is the *bust of Agrippina*. Its Baroque character is underlined by the folds of the ermine cape, in the knot of which notice the protuberant eyes and the tentacles of a giant squid, symbol of the empress' depravity. Agrippina's gaze is brooding and unsettling: she seems almost to sense her imminent murder by order of her son Nero.

THE FIELD OF MARS AND ITS MONUMENTS

In the first years of the life of the city, this area was covered by shrubby swamps. The Swan Canal and the Red Canal were dug along the along the western border of the area in order to drain it. It was here that Peter I's troops conducted their maneuvers and here that on holidays the "amusement lights" (fireworks) were set off: for this reason the huge square was originally called the Amusement Field.

As time went on, elegant palaces were built along the perimeter of the square: to the west the palace built by Elizabeth, Peter I's daughter; to the south that built by Catherine, Peter's wife. The square thus changed name and became the Czarinas' Meadow.

The *Saltykov Mansion*, designed by G. Quarenghi, was built in 1784-1788 in the northeastern portion of the square on the banks of the Neva. Alongside it was then raised the *Beszkiy Palace* (architect unknown), a building on the banks of the Neva and the Swan Canal—the garden on the roof of which, with turrets at the corners, caught the attention of the passersby of the time.

The square was given its current name in the 18th-19th centuries, when the monuments to the Russian military leaders A. Suvorov and P. Rumianzev were installed. The obelisk to Rumianzev's victory was transferred, at C. Rossi's suggestion, to Vasilevskiy Island. The *monument to Alexander Suvorov*, who victoriously engaged Napoleon's troops, was inaugurated on 5 May 1801, the first anniversary of his death, and is a masterpiece among Russian monuments. The sculptor M. Kozlovskiy, whose aspiration was not faithful portraiture but expression of Suvorov's military genius, his courage, and his indomitable will, portrayed him in the guise of the god Mars.

The decision to build here the *barracks of the Pavlovskiy Guards Regiment* (which had heroically fought against Napoleon's armies) was made in 1812. The barracks buildings, designed by the architect Vasiliy Stasov, were raised in 1817-1819 along the western side of the Field of Mars. The extremely wide facade, featuring three porticoes of Ionic columns, dominates the Field of Mars; the

On these pages, the Pavlovskiy Regiment building, details of the facade, and the monument to Alexander Suvorov.

decorations—weapons and armor—only stress the function of the building, which is one of the finest creations of Russian Classicism.

In 1919 the **Monument to Revolutionary Fighters** was installed at the center of the Field of Mars: it is square in form and made of granite. Since 1957 an eternal flame has burned here.

The Venice of the North

S aint Petersburg is often called the Venice of the North. And in fact it does recall the jewel of the Adriatic Sea, even though Venice is situated on 118 islands in a lagoon while Saint Petersburg counts only 44. In 1861, geographers ascertained that the city was set on 101 islands, but since then many watercourses have been earthed in, several rivers have dried up, and many of the islands have joined together.

The sea, rivers, canals, islands, and islets, therefore—and bridges with "colorful" names (Blue Bridge, Red Bridge, Green Bridge . . .) and elegant foot-bridges—but also balustrades that speak of Burano lace woven with iron, studded with fine palaces that reflect in the salt and fresh waters recall (though in other forms and with a different history) the palaces along the Canal Grande; and then, doesn't the bridge over the Winter Canal have something in common with Venice's Ponte dei Sospiri? And yet, even with so many similar features, if we look closely the two cities are different, each unique, each with its own character, its own personality. The

Venice of the North—it was said—but also the Pearl of the Baltic. But in truth, the ancient, unmistakable, superb capital of the czars is best called simply by its own name: **Saint Petersburg**.

Buildings along the Moyka river with the Pushkin House-Museum in the foreground and the plaque recalling the poet's death.

On the facing page, the Pushkin House-Museum: the great poet's study and the garden with his commemorative statue.

THE MOYKA RIVER

ALEXANDER PUSHKIN HOUSE-MUSEUM

A marble plaque on the wall at No. 12 of the Moyka Embankment tells us that Alexander Pushkin died in this house on 29 January 1837. The house, built in the 1720's, was restructured in 1770-1780 and in 1909-1910 its layout was considerably modified. But in 1806 it passed into the hands of the Volkonskiy family of princes.

In 1835 the property passed to the princess Sofia Volkonskaya (sister of Sergei Volkonskiy, one of the organizers of the Decembrist movement). Pushkin rented "the whole first ground floor, composed of eleven rooms" in the fall of 1836 and moved in in September: it was his sixth home in the capital. He lived there for only four and one-half months and it was here that he died following his duel with Dantès. Vasiliy Zhukovskiy, Pushkin's oldest friend, drew up a detailed plan of the house at the time; although the house was later rebuilt, the plans have permitted recreating its aspect during the period of Pushkin's tenancy; Pushkin's friends made an effort to preserve the poet's personal effects, and thanks to these facts, in 1925, it was possible to create one of the first Pushkin museums in the apartment on the Moyka.

The Pushkin House-Museum has recreated the wood stoves, the central staircase, the parquet floors, and the cornices decorated with stuccowork, and has refurbished the colors of the walls, the curtains, and the draperies. The museum counts eight rooms: the pantry, the dining room, the sitting room, the bedrooms, the rooms of Pushkin's wife's sisters (Alexandra and Catherine Goncharov), the childrens' room, the poet's studio, and the entranceway. The items on exhibit include various mementos, like the last portrait for which Pushkin

Duel for Honor

The behavior of the monarchist French official Georges Dantès, who brashly courted Pushkin's wife, was taken as a pretext by the poet's enemies near the czar's throne to torment him by spreading the false charges that offended the honor of both the Pushkin and his wife. The upshot of the duel that followed was tragic for Pushkin. Mortally wounded, he was carried to this house on the Moyka—and here, in his study, on a couch surrounded by shelves of books, Russia's greatest poet died on 29 January (10 February) 1837. News of his death spread like lightning through the capital and a multitude of people of all ages and social conditions came to his home to pay homage to the mortal remains of the well-loved writer.

sat, the portrait of his wife, the vest worn by the poet at the duel, the medallion, a lock of his hair, and much more.

Among the items that belonged to Pushkin are his desk and armchair, the inkwell with the bronze figure of a Moorish boy (a gift of one of the poet's closest friends), and his cane with a button from Peter the Great's jacket set in its handle. Pushkin's library (4500 volumes) includes classics of world literature, books on geography, history, astronomy, economy, and chess theory, as well as dictionaries, vademecums, and mementos. Pushkin knew French, Italian, Spanish, Latin, English, and German to perfection and his books have been published in scores of languages. The original books in his library are held by the Russian Language Institute of the Academy of Sciences; the volumes in the museum are copies.

Two images of the majestic New Holland arch.

NEW HOLLAND

At the time of Peter I, the western portion of the island hosting the Admiralty (between the Neva and the Moyka) was the capital's workers' suburb and the Admiralty shipyard and the other secondary shipyards were located here. The watercourses crossing in the area had created a triangular island called New Holland even in Peter's time, since many features reminded the czar of his beloved Netherlands. It was decided to build sheds on the island to store ship timber; design of the complex was entrusted to the architect Savva Cevakinskiy; of the facades to J. Vallin de la Mothe. Cevakinskiy proposed building the sheds in such a manner that their function be not purely productive but also to incorporate a certain architectural value; he also called for construction of a huge arch that was built in 1770-1779 to plans by Vallin de la Mothe.

At the sides of this commanding arch (23 meters tall) were raised buildings ranging in height from 13 to 17 meters. The New Holland arch is one of the most impressive constructions. The commanding paired columns that flank the arch are made of blocks of red granite; in granite also the column bases and capitals. Between one column and another are niches of severe design, decorated with sculpted garlands in light gray stone. The same material was used for the medallions above the niches.

The arch rests on small granite columns, on the banks of the channel that leads from the Moyka into New Holland.

YUSUPOV PALACE

In 1830, Prince N. Yusupov purchased the two-story house at No. 94 of the Moyka Embankment and had it entirely rebuilt (1830-1836) by the architect Andrey Mikhaylov. Particularly important, from the architectural and artistic points of view—in the interior—are the lovely **Hall of the White Columns**, the ballroom, the **Great Rotunda**, and the **Red and Blue Rooms**, the walls of which were clad in imitation marble and covered in damask; also of note are the ceilings, decorated by the premier artists of the period, the doors ornamented with gilded bronze armor, and the beautifully-designed parquet floors in precious woods. In 1858 the architect I. Monighetti rebuilt the main staircase, renovated the **palace theater** (180 seats), decorating it with gilded Baroque reliefs, and furnished the ground-floor rooms. In the fashion of the times, the owner ordered the **Turkish Study** and the **Mauritanian Room**; there is no suitable adjective for the latter but luxurious: it contained a marble fountain, the walls were clad in white marble with inlays of black and red mastic and gilt strips. Higher up on the walls were painted phrases in Arabic on glided backgrounds.

The theater was the venue for famous artists; in 1836 it hosted the première performance of the first act of Glinka's *A Life for the Czar*, with the composer one of the actors.

In 1919 the building came under State protection as a Neo-Classical monument and a repository of treasures of art, history, and culture.

In the cellars, in December 1916, Felix Yusupov, with the aid of Prince Dmitri (a relative of Czar Nicholas II) and the participation of the monarchist V. Purishkevich, Lieutenant Sukhotin, and Doctor Lazarev, succeeded in murdering the infamous **Grigoriy Rasputin**. Rasputin and his followers appointed and unseated ministers, governors, and commanders; they influenced the course of the war efforts and all government policies. Instances regarding Rasputin's behavior and prerogatives were more than once brought before the State Duma (Russian parliament), but by the czar's order the Minister of the Interior prohibited the newspapers from writing about Rasputin—or even mentioning his name. On the ground floor and in the cellars, *wax statues* provide a suggestive reconstruction of the story of the plot and Rasputin's murder.

Rasputin

Grigoriy Rasputin—whom today we might define a "mystic"—had an almost hypnotic influence over the czar and the czarina, who were convinced that his prayers could save Aleksei, the heir to the throne, suffering from hemophilia. The political circles that wanted to save the monarchy from ruin by eliminating Rasputin came up with the idea of having him assassinated; one of the first to express this idea was the 26-year-old Prince Yusupov, but the task was anything but simple: Rasputin was protected by 24 policemen. Yusupov invited Rasputin to his palace, promising that he would have introduced him to his wife, the beautiful Irina (who at that moment was out of town). Rasputin was offered sweets containing huge doses of poison, and also poisoned wine. But to no effect. It took the pistols of Yusupov and the other conspirators to finish him.

The facade of the Yusupov Palace on the Moyka.

The Griboedov Canal

MARIINSKIY THEATER

Erected in 1860 by Albert Kavos in 1860, and named in honor of the czarina Maria, wife of Alexander II, this is the city's premier opera and dance theater; it is also one of the world's best-known theaters for its ballet company. Many Russian works debuted in this theater; for example, Mussorgsky's *Boris Godunov* and Tchaikovsky's *Queen of Spades*.

The Neo-Renaissance exterior is a lovely pale blue against which white columns and reliefs stand out beautifully; the facade was restructured in 1883-1896 by the architect Viktor Schröter, who also designed the decoration.

The interior is dazzlingly sumptuous: all light blue and gold, with twisted columns, cherubs, medallions, and sparkling garlands. The superb stage curtain dates to 1914, the golden era of the Ballets Russes.

The griffins on Bank Bridge and the monument to Mikhail Glinka in front of the Mariinskiy Theater.

BANK BRIDGE

Since 1826, this lovely footbridge has united the two banks of the canal near a banking institution. This suspended bridge, one of the city's most beautiful, is supported by cables secured in the mouths of artistic **griffins** with gilded wings.

The **Lion Bridge**, another, similar footbridge again over the Griboedov Canal, was built in 1825-1826. Not far from here, past the curve in the canal, is the square with the Mariinskiy Theater, the Rimsky-Korsakov State Conservatory, and the Rimsky-Korsakov State Opera and Ballet Theater, where even the great Caruso performed.

The Mariinskiy Theater.

Russian Ballet and the Ballets Russes

Russian ballet, famous throughout the world, was born in this city in 1738, when the master Jean-Baptiste Landé, a Frenchman, opened a school of dance for the children of those working at the palace. Many foreign dance-masters taught at the school, which was called the Imperial Ballet School: the most important, perhaps, was Marius Petipa, who came to Saint Petersburg in 1847 as a dance, and later went on to become the choreographer of scores of ballets. The distaste for Classicism that arose after the 1905 Revolution led many artists to abandon the imperial theaters and join private companies like Sergei Diaghilev's famous Ballets Russes, the star of which was Vaslaw Nijinsky. Defection of artists continued under the Soviet regime; only Agrippina Vaganova, star ballerina, remained to train the new generations of dancers: hers is in fact the name of the Vaganova Ballet School, sited in the prestigious Ulitsa Zodchevo Rossi.

Portrait of Sergej Diaghilev and images of ballets at the Mariinskiy Theater: The Nutcracker *and* The Fall of the Gods.

Natalia Razina

Natalia Razina

Saint Nicholas' Cathedral and its bell tower overlooking the Kryukov Canal.

SAINT NICHOLAS' CATHEDRAL

The church, named for the patron saint of sailors, overlooks the point where the waters of the Griboedov Canal mix with those of the Kryukov Canal. It was built in 1753-1762 to plans by the architect Savva Chevakinskiy, who decorated the exterior with Corinthian columns; five gilded domes rise above the magnificent Baroque building. The lovely four-story bell tower topped by a gilded spire soars above the green park of the cathedral, near the Kryukov Canal.

The cathedral hosts two churches, according to Russian tradition: the lower church, destined for daily services, has interesting 18th-century icons by the Kolokolnikov brothers and is theatrically lighted by candles and chandeliers; the upper church, in which the Sunday and feast-day services are celebrated, is more luminous and decorated with gilded Baroque stuccowork and a marvelous carved wooden iconostasis.

Saint Nicholas' Cathedral is also known as the "Sailors' Church" since it was built for the sailors and employees of the Admiralty who lived in the area.

THE FONTANKA RIVER

SHEREMETEV PALACE (FONTANNYY HOUSE)

Today's stone building was ordered by the son of Field Marshal Boris Sheremetev, who had received as a gift from Peter I a parcel of land on the east bank of the Fontanka: in 1750-1755 the architects S. Cevakinskiy and F. Argunov created the building that is also known as *Fontannyy dom*, or Fountain House, due to the many fountains present on the estate.

The plan of the palace recalls the Anichkov Palace complex. The vast park behind the building was adorned with a Chinese-style kiosk, a grotto, and various pavilions. The central portion of the facade is highlighted by a mezzanine and a semicircular pediment, while the ends of the facade are adorned with two triangular pediments. The Corinthian pilasters and the sculptural ornamentation place the Sheremetev Palace among the best of Saint Petersburg's examples of Baroque architectural style.

In the 1840's, a beautiful wrought-iron *grille* on a granite base, with decorative details in gilded bronze (all designed by I. Corsini), was erected to separate the palace from the river esplanade. In 1867, an annex and the gates with the **Sheremetev coat-of-arms** were built to plans by N. Benois. The extremely rich owners are the subject of an exhibit in the palace, which is the home of the **State Theater and Music Museum**. The **Anna Akhmatova Museum** is instead located in the service wing of the palace in which the great woman poet lived at length.

ANICHKOV BRIDGE

The Anichkov Bridge is famous for the four *equestrian sculptures* by Pyotr Klodt: all four groups portray young men who in various manners and poses attempt to tame wild horses.

What we see are copies; the originals are in Naples and Berlin.

THE TRINITY CATHEDRAL OF THE IZMAILOVSKY REGIMENT

The Trinity Cathedral of the Izmailovsky Regiment, on the left bank of the Fontanka, has five blue domes decorated with stars. It was built in 1828-1835 by Stasov, a monument to whom stands alongside the church.

Sheremetev Palace, with its lovely grille, one of the four sculptural groups on the Anichkov Bridge, and the Trinity Cathedral of the Izmailovsky Regiment.

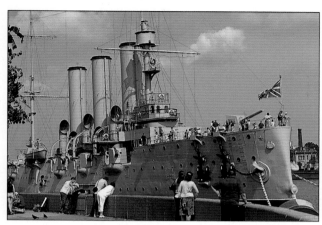

THE CRUISER *AURORA*

Anchored in front of the Naval Academy on the Great Nevka, the historical battle cruiser *Aurora*, now a **floating museum**, attracts numerous visitors. More than once at the center of history-making events (like when, in 1908, its crew were the first to aid the population of Messina after the earthquake), its fame is inextricably linked to the Revolution. On the night of 7 November (25 October) the cruiser sailed up the Neva and at a signal from the Naryshkin bastion fired the cannon shot that started the attack on the Winter Palace.

The monument to Saint Alexander Nevsky in the square of the same name in front of the entrance to the "Lavra."

On the facing page, the artistic contrast of colors and styles between the red Baroque forms of the Church of the Annunciation and the yellow Neo-Classical lines of the Trinity Cathedral.

THE SAINT ALEXANDER NEVSKY "LAVRA"

This one of the city's oldest architectural complexes is located at the end of the Nevskiy Prospekt. The Alexander Nevsky Monastery was founded in 1710 by order of Peter I on the site believed to be that of the 1240 Battle of the Neva, when the Prince of Novgorod Alexander Nevsky ("Nevsky" means "of the Neva") defeated the Swedes. Peter I named the monastery thus in honor of the canonization of the prince, patriot, and military leader. The status of *Lavra*, a term indicating a highly-regarded monastery accorded various privileges, was conferred in 1797 by Czar Paul I.

In Russia, the monasteries have always been centers of learning and culture. In 1726, the school attended mainly by the sons of ministers was opened at the Alexander Nevsky Monastery. Subjects included penmanship, grammar, arithmetic, the Scriptures, prayers, etc. Today the monastery is the seat of the Seminary and the Theological Academy of the Russian Orthodox Church; both institutions offer four-year courses.

The enclosure of the monastic complex delimits a broad semicircle on **Alexander Nevsky Square** at the end of the Nevskiy Prospekt. On the arched central entrance over the monastery gates is Church of the Holy Mother of God erected in 1783-1785 to Ivan Starov's designs. Two monumental cemeteries lie to the left and the right of the main entrance. The monastic complex as such rises across the Monastyrka stream; it is vaguely trapezoidal in form with the longest side toward the Neva; its construction was supervised by the architects Domenico Trezzini and Ivan Starov.

Church of the Annunciation

To the left of the main entrance is the oldest building in the monastic complex—the Church of the Annunciation. Completed in 1722, it houses a number of tombs including that of Suvorov and those of various statesmen and generals of the 1700's and 1800's and members of the imperial family. Many of the sepulchers in the church feature stones created by I. Martos, F. Gordeev, and other famous sculptors.

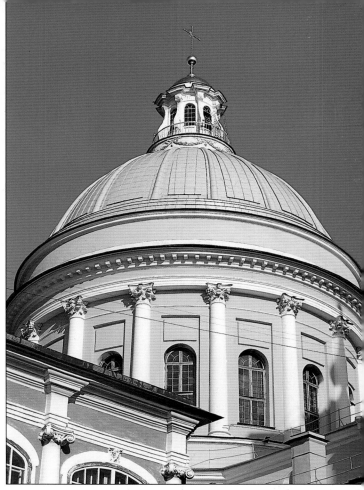

Views of the monastery complex and the interior of Trinity Cathedral.

Vladimir Melnikov

Trinity Cathedral

The Neo-Classical Trinity Cathedral, with its two bell towers, one to each side of the facade, stands out in the prevalently Baroque-style monastery complex. At the center of the side of the monastery facing the Neva, it was built by order of Catherine II in 1776-1790 to plans by Ivan Starov (with sculptural decorations by F. Shubin). The sumptuous interior of the monastery's main church abounds in precious marbles; the iconostasis in red agate and white marble features wonderful pictorial works. The mortal remains of Alexander Nevsky, Russia's patron saint, are preserved in a reliquary to the right of the iconostasis.

At the center of the opposite side of the monastic complex is the **Metropolitan's House** (also called the House of the Archpriest) built in the 1750's by the architect M. Rastorguiev. The elegant building stands out among the other constructions in the complex for its redundant decoration. The columns and pillars create a delicate play of chiaroscuro.

Southwest of the monastery is the **Seminary** building, also lavishly decorated and also built by M. Rastorguiev in the same period as the Metropolitan's House.

The Final Resting Places of Many Famous Personalities

Past the entrance arch of the Lavra complex are two cemeteries. Left of the entrance is the ancient **Lazarevsky Cemetery** founded in 1716 only shortly after the monastery when Princess Nathalie, Peter the Great's sister, was buried here.

This cemetery is the final resting place of important figures in Russian culture, such as M. Lomonosov, D. Fonvisin, G. Quarenghi, I. Starov, A. Voronikhin, A. Zakharov, C. Rossi, F. Shubin, and M. Kozlovsky.

Right of the entrance is the **Tikhvinsky Cemetery**. On the tombstones we read the names of the poet I. Krylov, the musicians M. Glinka, P. Tchiaikovsky, M. Mussorgsky, N. Rimsky-Korsakov, the painter A. Ivanov, the writer F. Dostoevsky, the architect V. Stasov, the sculptor Pyotr Klodt, the Soviet scientist (inventor of synthetic rubber) S. Lebedev, and the brilliant Soviet actress E. Korchagina-Alexandrovskaya.

1. M. Lomonosov
2. N. Rimsky-Korsakov
3. I. Krylov
4. M. Glinka
5. M. Mussorgsky
6. P. Tchiaikovsky
7. F. Dostoevsky

A view of the Smolnyy Monastery with the Cathedral of
the Resurrection and the Neo-Classical facade of the
Smolnyy Institute.

THE SMOLNYY CONVENT AND INSTITUTE

Here, Rastrelli's Baroque and Quarenghi's Neo-Classicism combine to create a harmonious architectural ensemble.

In 1749, B. F. Rastrelli, master of an unmistakable Baroque style that mixed Russian and Western elements for extraordinary decorative effects, began construction of a majestic complex: a closed square with the cathedral at the center. The architecture is as sumptuous as that of later civil buildings by the same author.

The **Cathedral of the Resurrection** dominates the complex and the surrounding urban area: the panoramic view from the right bank of the Neva is of great effect. Flanking the tambour that supports the central dome, which rises to a height of 85 meters, are four elegant bell towers. This five-dome solution is clearly inspired by the ancient Russian monasteries. The austere white interior of the cathedral contrasts with the light blue and the imaginative Baroque of the exterior. Rastrelli's designs called for a 140-meter tower in front of the cathedral; for lack of funds, it was never built.

When she ascended the throne, Catherine II founded, in the unfinished convent building, the "Society for the Further Education of Noblewomen in Russia," the country's first public school for the daughters of noble families.

Institute for Young Noblewomen

Alongside the cathedral and the monastery was built (1806-1808) a charitable institution for older women and the needy widows "of the public officials of the czar." This work by Quarenghi, known throughout the world as the "Smolnyy," features a wide facade (about 220 meters) broken by the arches of the center entrance and surmounted by a portico with eight Ionic columns. The interiors are even more severe. Of all the many rooms, only the enormous **great hall** is of real interest: with two orders of windows, it occupies the second and third floors of the south wing and is framed by a solemn colonnade; its decoration includes a frieze around the walls and chandeliers.

When Quarenghi completed the building it became the home of the Smolnyy Institute for Young Noblewomen (about 200); the monastery then hosted the hospice.

The Institute was suppressed in August 1917; it was from here that Lenin, whose statue stands in front of the entrance, directed the Bolshevik coup.

Fabergé and the Czars' "Golden Eggs"

"Spring Egg"

Fortune, for Peter Carl Fabergé—jeweler at the Romanov court—arrived in the form of an Easter egg. Czar Alexander III had requested the young court goldsmith to create a special jewel as an Easter gift to the czarina Maria Fyodorovna.

It is said that Fabergé didn't come out of his workshop in Bolshaya Morskaya for weeks, promising the czar that the gift would have been exceptional. It is also said that the czar was quite deluded when what he saw was an Easter egg: in gold, sure enough, but simply an Easter egg. But when the czarina opened it, she discovered the exceptional surprise that Fabergé had promised his ruler: inside the egg was a golden yolk containing a tiny (also golden) hen; inside it, a copy in miniature of the Imperial diamond-studded crown; and inside this, a miniature ruby egg. The czar was so impressed that, from that year onward, he ordered a Fabergé Easter Egg each year.

In truth, the adventure that brought Peter Carl Faberge to the city began much earlier, in 1686, when his family of Huguenot origin left Picardy to escape the persecutions that ensued after the Louis XIV revoked the Edict of Nantes. After years—and more—of traveling through northern Europe, the family finally settled in Saint Petersburg, where in 1842 Gustav Fabergé began working as a goldsmith and jeweler. It was here that on 30 May 1846 Peter Carl was born. He was instructed in his father's craft and educated in the European tradition of the best goldsmiths of the time. In 1870, when he was just twenty-four, he took over his father's business—and from that moment on, relaunched and developed it.

After his first success with Alexander III, the tradition of the golden eggs grew; and even expanded: when in 1896 Nicholas II ascended the throne, the Easter Egg tradition doubled, since the new czar decided to present two each Easter, one to his wife and one to his mother. And thus, from that time until 1917, Fabergé produced 57 eggs, not only for the Russian imperial family which had decreed his fame—other crowned heads of Europe also ordered eggs.

"Coronation"

But why an egg? The Orthodox Easter celebration, in Russia, was considered to be the year's most important and the tradition of making gifts of colored eggs—real or manufactured as they may have been—reflected thousands of years of craftsmanship.

We might well say, then, that the imperial Easter eggs were not only masterpieces of the goldsmiths' art but the never-forgotten and highest expression of a centuries'-old custom in the great Russian world.

1897 was the year of the most famous of the eggs Fabergé created for his ruler: his masterpiece, the "Coronation Egg." Closed it is superb: in red gold, wrapped in a net of laurel leaves, each crossing marked by the two-headed imperial eagle in black enamel and diamonds. Open, it is astounding: a perfect replica of the coach used by Nicholas and Alexandra for the coronation. It is made of yellow gold and enamel, topped by the crown and six imperial eagles, and is perfectly functional—opening the doors lowers the steps!

More "intimate" the egg produced for the 15th anniversary of the coronation of Nicholas II: what strikes us most this time is not its opulence but the fact that the oval portraits are of the czar, the czarina, and their 5 children. In 1917, this world and all its people disappeared. And Peter Carl Fabergé, exiled from his country, died in Lausanne in 1920.

"Lilies of the Valley"

"Fifteenth Anniversary"

Chesma Church

This highly unusual church stands in the south part of the city, a little more than five kilometers from the historical center of Saint Petersburg, on a side street to the east of the Moskovskiy Prospekt.

According to a legend narrated, the Finnish once called this area the "frog marsh." Catherine II met the messenger who was bringing news of Russia's June 1770 victory over the Turks at Chesma Bay. In honor of the historical event, the empress had a palace built on the site of the encounter, while the church was built only some years afterwards (in truth, the Chesma Palace was built as a stopover point for Catherine when she traveled to and from Tsarskoe Selo).

The more-than-once reconstructed and restored Chesma Church is one of the few Neo-Gothic buildings in Saint Petersburg. It was built in 1777-1780 to plans by the architect Yuriy Velten, also the author of the palace.

The external walls of the church, an unmistakable brick red and broken by tall lancet-arched windows, are decorated with narrow white vertical molding strips. These are interrupted by a series of blind ogival arches and continue on to form a sort of crown circling the entire building.

During the Communist era the church was used as a museum commemorating the battle whose name it bears; it is now again used as a place of worship.

The unique Chesma Church in Neo-Gothic style.

Piskarevskoe Memorial Cemetery

The northeastern suburb of Saint Petersburg is home to the Piskarevskoe Memorial Cemetery, laid out on 26 hectares and designed by the architects E. Levinson and A. Vassilyev.

The—however summary—introduction outlines how things went during the war and how dramatic was the siege of the city. The dead were originally buried in different cemeteries, but beginning on 15 February 1942 only in the common grave near the town of Piskarevka. The Piskarevskoe Memorial Cemetery is the final resting place of almost five hundred thousand people who died in the years 1941-1943.

The fence around the cemetery runs for many hundreds of meters. At the two sides of the entrance are two pavilions, with strictly geometric forms that recall the Greek propylaea. The friezes of the pavilions are engraved with words in memory of the deeds of those who took part in Saint Petersburg's drama. Inside the pavilion is an exhibit of documents relating to the Siege of what was then Leningrad, with a map of the besieged city and the statements of patriot volunteers who fought the invader. Also presented is a tragic document known worldwide: the diary of the eleven-year-old Tanya Saviceva. Almost every page of the diary speaks of death by starving of a member of the large Savicev family. This sad list ends with the words, "The Savicev's have died. They're all dead. Tanya is now alone." (Tanya Saviceva was evacuated from Leningrad in serious condition, and did not survive the experience: she died well behind the front).

Many photographs immortalize the work of the drivers who plied the "Lifeline" over the ice of Lake Ladozhskoe. In 152 days (from 22 November 1941 through 24 April 1942): 104 vehicles disappeared underneath the ice broken by Hitler's shells and bombs—and most of them carried men or goods.

Behind the pavilions opens a vast plaza over the cemetery territory. At the center burns an eternal flame in a cornice of shiny black stone. To the left is a pond, the bottom of which is lined with granite and decorated with mosaics of an oak branch and a lighted torch. Granite steps lead down from the terrace toward the central avenue, lined with mounds, each with a granite slab. The stones are engraved with oak leaves and a date (1941 or 1942 or 1943) and hammer and sickle or a red star to indicate whether those interred are civilians or soldiers who fell in battle.

The central plaza, 300 meters long by 75 in width, is tree-lined. At the very end is a wall with verses by Olga Bergholts, herself a survivor of the siege. The granite of the wall is sculpted with the figures of the military and the civilians who defended Saint Petersburg: soldiers, sailors, volunteers, women laying flowers on the tombs of the fallen. At the sides of the bas-relief are flags draped in black and overturned torches, symbols of life winking out. And then, four kneeling figures: Woman, Worker, Soldier, and Sailor, symbolizing the entire population in mourning.

The center of the Memorial composition is a female figure representing Mother Russia (sculptors V. Isayeva and R. Taurit).

ENVIRONS

amous throughout the world, the environs of Saint Petersburg are localities that are true pearls scattered in a semicircle south of the city. Even Peter I was well aware that a capital that wanted to compete in magnificence with the great European centers had to have a palace outside the city itself.

*And thus it was that beginning with Peter, the Russian czars and czarinas took turns building marvelous palaces and enchanting gardens on the outskirts of the city. **Petrodvorets-Peterhof, Tsarskoe Selo-Pushkin, Pavlovsk, Oranienbaum-Lomonosov,** and **Gatchina** are therefore not-to-be-missed complements to any visit to the former capital of the czars.*

Petrodvorets - Peterhof

The history of this locality on the southern coast of the Gulf of Finland, 29 kilometers from Saint Petersburg, goes back to the early 18th century. Petrodvorets-Peterhof ("Peter's court") was conceived by Peter the Great as a monument to victory by Russia, which had always sought an outlet on the Baltic—and in fact all the decorative elements tend to glorify Russia as a maritime power. Czar Peter I, who went into raptures when he visited Versailles, was determined to make Peterhof a more beautiful holding than the French kings'. The task was anything but simple, however, since all the land had to be reclaimed.

Design was entrusted to Jean Baptiste Le Blonde, who built the Great Palace and the enormous expanse of park and gardens (more than 600 hectares). The palace, inaugurated in 1723, was enlarged by Rastrelli for the

Empress Elizabeth and later modified by Yuriy Velten for Catherine the Great.

The Peterhof estate counts a great number of buildings, pavilions, and three parks: the Upper Gardens, the Lower Gardens, and the Alexandria Park, all adorned with fountains, tree-shaded boulevards, and paths through woodland areas.

The **Great Palace**, with its 250-meter facade, contains marvelous works like Rastrelli's Baroque **Main Staircase**, the **Throne Room** redesigned by Yuriy Velten in 1770, and the **Imperial Suite**, including Peter I's original (and perfectly-preserved) Oak Study.

Besides the Great Palace, to the sides of which rise the elegant buildings called *"for the cult"* and *"under the arms,"* the estate counts a number of other constructions like the **Monplaisir Palace**, with its notable *Ceremonial*

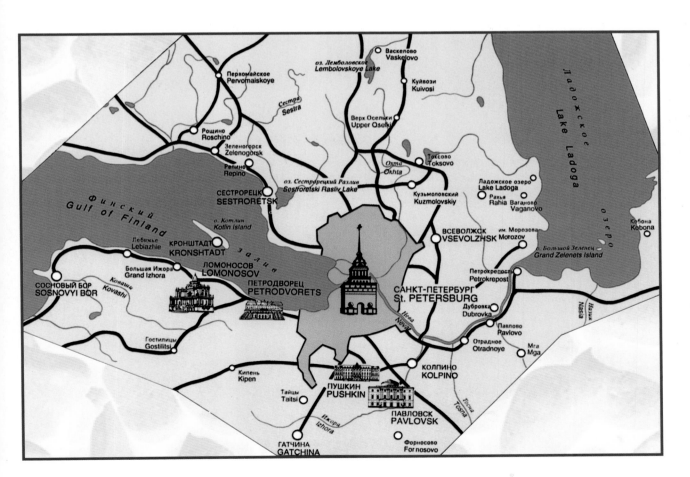

Hall, facing the Gulf of Finland; the **Marly Palace**, a well-proportioned country residence for the czar's guests; the **Hermitage Pavilion**, on the shores of the gulf, designed for private dining by the czar and his guests; and the Neo-Gothic **Cottage Palace** in the Alexandria Park.

Petrodvorets, however, is also known for its many artistic fountains and cascades, adorned with gilded bronze statues and featuring imaginative plays of water. The stunning **Grand Cascade**, with the **Samson Fountain**, in practice unites the Great Palace and the Baltic Sea through the **Marine Canal**. Other fountains of note, many of which are located in the lower portion of the park (toward the sea), are the **Neptune Fountain**, the **Adam Fountain** and the similar one with a statue of **Eve**, the **Pyramid Fountain**, and the **Roman Fountains**.

At the entrance to Petrodvorets, on the main avenue, stands the Cathedral of Saints Peter and Paul built in 1895-1904 to designs by N. Sultanov, in the Muscovite masonry style. It is in red brick, pyramidal in form, and crowned by five polygonal domes topped by the typical gilded "onion" cupolas.

The Cathedral of Saints Peter and Paul at the entrance to Petrodvorets (top) and the Great Palace with the lovely Grand Cascade.
Below, the "under the arms" building, behind one of the park's many fountains.

Rastrelli's sparkling Main Staircase.

Right, the Triton Fountain.

On these pages, the Throne Room in the Great Palace.

Tsarskoe Selo - Pushkin

Tsarskoe Selo—that is, the "Village of the Czar"—is made up of a whole complex of quite unusual palaces and parks, the work of renowned Russian and European architects of the 18th and 19th centuries. In 1937 this locality was given the name of Alexander Pushkin, Russia's greatest poet.

In 1710 ownership of the area, by the czar's wish, passed to Peter's wife, the future Empress Catherine I. The palace, construction of which had just begun, was dedicated to her. During the reign of Elizabeth (1741-1761) the palace was repeatedly renovated by various Russian architects. In 1762, the great specialist in Baroque architecture, Francesco Bartolomeo Rastrelli, was called in to modernize the palace, and he linked all the single parts of the building to form a coherent whole. The renovated palace was much taller, with main facades 325 meters long. An enormous number of columns and statues and a quantity of decorative stuccos adorned the deep blue walls of the facades. For gilding the statues and the other decorative elements, 105.242 kilograms of gold were used. Rastrelli adorned the Court of Honor in front of the palace with marvelous gilded iron railings. One of the palace's most outstanding features was the Amber Room, the panels of which were created for Friedrich Wilhelm I of Prussia who in 1716 gave them to Peter the Great in exchange for 248 Herculean soldiers for the Royal Guard.

The palace suffered serious damage during World War II. The fires destroyed treasures of inestimable value; an infinite number of works of art were barbarously disfigured or removed, like the entire Amber Room; a multitude of centuries-old trees were chopped down in the old parks and explosions destroyed pavilions and statues. After the Liberation (24 January 1944) the scholars, historians, and restorers began their patient and painstaking work with the aim of rebuilding the palaces and parks in order to recreate the original authentic aspect of Tsarskoe Selo.

The **Great Staircase** was built to the architect Ippolito Monighetti's designs in 1860. It is right at the center of the palace and occupies the entire space between the west and east sides. The white marble stairs and the decorative cups and vases in Japanese and Chinese porcelain exalt the solemn atmosphere of the

The glittering domes of the Royal Chapel in Catherine's palace at Tsarskoe Selo.

The Great Pond with the Admiralty Pavilion.

Catherine's opulent Imperial Palace.

interiors. The ceiling decorations are the work of 17th-18th century Italian painters. At the center is a marvelous *Judgement of Paris*. The **Cavaliers' Dining Room**, designed by Rastrelli, destroyed during World War II and later faithfully reconstructed, is a phantasmagoria of sculptures, garlands, and gilded shells that reflect, multiplying to infinity, in the mirrors. The same play of reflections characterizes the **Great Hall** or **Throne Room**. One of the most elegant rooms in the palace is the **Blue Drawing Room**, by the Scotsman Charles Cameron, in which soft tones of blue and

green predominate. The park is punctuated by pools, canals, bridges, fountains, artificial grottoes, and many buildings; for example, the **Turkish Bath**, the **Admiralty Pavilion**, and the **Creaking Pavilion**. The **Alexander Palace**, one of Giacomo Quarenghi's masterpieces, stands in an adjacent park.

From top to bottom, the Blue Drawing Room, the sparkling Great Hall or Throne Room, the Cavaliers' Dining Room,

The main facade of the central portion of the palace and the State Bedroom.

Pavlovsk

The park at Pavlovsk extends over 600 hectares, within which areas with geometrical layouts alternate with other areas left in their natural state. The harmony among the parts depends partially on the sheer size of Pavlovsk, but also on the bizarre course of the Slavyanka river and the sequence of undulations and plains that characterize the terrain. The **Great Palace**—or **Paul's Palace**—is the compositive fulcrum of the vast park in which it is immersed, and its profile is visible even from the farthest corners of the estate. Many architects contributed to creating the palace and the park, but the predominant style is Cameron's Neo-Classicism.

The building unites monumentality and airiness: two curving wings flanking the central portion close in a near-circle before this "Palladian mansion." Sixty-four closely-set white columns support the flat dome that tops the building. The ground floor resembles a monumental plinth on which the first and second floors rest; the first floor hosts the ceremonial halls. While on the northwest side (facing the Slavyanka river) the Great Palace would seem to be a stupendous country manor, from the southeast side (the main entrance) the solemnity of the aspect of the building makes one suspect it might have been Czar Paul's official residence. The interior boasts a number of variously-decorated, and all quite elegant, rooms, including the *Egyptian Vestibule*, the *Italian Hall* with its beautiful chandelier by Russian craftsmen, the *Rossi Library* designed by the architect of the same name*, Paul I's Library*, *Maria Fyodorovna's Library*, the *State Bedroom*, the *Palace Chapel*, and the *Greek Hall*. In the park we find the **Rose Pavilion**, the **Three Graces Pavilion**, the **Centaur Bridge**, the **Temple of Friendship**, the **Visconti Bridge**, the **Apollo Colonnade**, the **Cold Baths Pavilion**, and the **Étoile**, the first "English garden" area of the park, with its nine *statues of the Muses* set in a circle.

Maria Fyodorovna's Library and the Palace Chapel.

Oranienbaum-Lomonosov

The park of this estate—like all the others—hosts a number of buildings. The sumptuous **Menshikov Palace** or **Great Palace**, built by Czar Peter I's best friend and councilor, rivaled even the emperor's palace at Petrodvorets in sheer grandiosity. The Palace of Peter III is a modest residence of just two floors with four rooms on the ground floor and six smaller rooms above. The **Sliding Hill** (or Roller Coaster) **Pavilion**, on three floors, was the starting point for one of the sources of amusement at court: in practice, it was the start of a long inclined plane down which cars with metal wheels ran on rails. Unfortunately, all that remains today is the elegant pavilion from which they started.

The **Chinese Palace**, designed by Rinaldi, was Catherine the Great's "personal *dacha*": the **Rococo interiors** are enchanting, as are the *chinoiseries* so in vogue in her time.

In 1948, the estate was renamed Lomonosov in honor of the great 18th-century scholar—but the locality is still known by both names.

The elegant forms of the Chinese Palace reflected in one of the park's many ponds.

The Japanese Pavilion of the Great Palace.

The Sliding Hill Pavilion, a great source of amusement for the Imperial court and its guests.

Gatchina

The austere **Gatchina Palace**, ordered built by that Prince Orlov who was the lover of Catherine the Great, is unlike any other palace seen heretofore. The architect Rinaldi, charged with its creation, built it in simple and severe Neo-Classical forms—in sharp contrast, however, with the luxurious interiors.

At the death of the prince, the palace was given by Catherine to her son Paul, the future czar. He had it renovated by the architect Vittorio Brenna in line with his well-known tastes for all military; Brenna added a floor—and a moat with a drawbridge.

The palace was also the preferred residence of Alexander III, who moved in permanently with his whole family, deserting the state rooms and living in the more modest servants' quarters.

Although severely damaged during World War II and still subject of restoration work, the finest of the rooms are the **Marble Dining Room**, the **White Ballroom**, and **Paul I's bedroom** in one of the towers built by Brenna.

The grounds, abounding in water, afford the opportunity to boat on the lake and visit the buildings set there, like the **Priory Palace**, the **Temple of Venus** on the Island of Love, and the **Birch House**.

Gatchina Palace.

Vladimir Melnikov

INDEX